EDWARDIAN MINING IN OLD POSTCARDS

Petticoat Dan.

JOHN HANNAVY

First published in Great Britain in 2013

Copyright © John Hannavy 2013
www.johnhannavy.co.uk

Every attempt has been made by the author
to secure the appropriate permissions for
materials reproduced in this book. If there has
been any oversight we will be happy to rectify
the situation and a written submission should
be made to the Publishers.

British Library Cataloguing-in-Publication Data
A CIP record for this title is available from the
British Library

ISBN 978 0 85710 074 0

PiXZ Books
Halsgrove House, Ryelands Business Park,
Bagley Road, Wellington, Somerset TA21 9PZ
Tel: 01823 653777
Fax: 01823 216796
email: sales@halsgrove.com

An imprint of Halstar Ltd, part of the
Halsgrove group of companies
Information on all Halsgrove titles is
available at: www.halsgrove.com

Printed and bound in China by
Everbest Printing Co Ltd

Title page image: 'Petticoat Dan' Cooper of Kirkintilloch was an Edwardian coal-carrier, and something of a local celebrity. His story is told on pages 17.

Contents page image: A recently refurbished coal wagon from Douglas Bank Colliery near Wigan, photographed in the early 1900s. The original has been digitally tinted and framed to recreate the character of an Edwardian postcard. On the back of the original print is an account of the cost of repainting – 'for giving the wagon two coats of paint, 1 extra coat on new timber, lettering in white 2 coats, shading in black, and blacking all ironwork, 12/6d.' Seven men and three boys pose with their handiwork, the man on the right still holding his paint brush and white paint.

ACKNOWLEDGEMENTS
All illustrations are from the author's collection except the following, which are acknowledged, with thanks, as follows: Bob Allard, 114: the late Donald Anderson, 97, 118: Richard Crangle, 76: Mark Fynn (www.warnergothard.com), 14, 21, 96, 107-9, 111, 115-6. 119, 123: Richard Higgs, 14, 26-7(top), 36-41(top), 42(top), 43(bottom), 44, 50-54(top), 55-57(top), 63, 74-5, 111-3, 124: David and Marilyn Parkinson, 9, 27(bottom), 43, 61, 82-3, 89: the late Miss Olga Pimblett, 96, 126: Ludwig Vogl-Bienek, 34 left, 104 top:

All modern photographs © John Hannavy

CONTENTS

PREFACE

MY FASCINATION with Edwardian postcards of collieries, miners and pit brow lasses started nearly forty years ago when walking through a derelict printing works in Wigan, Lancashire. The works had been the production centre for one of Wigan's major postcard publishers, James Starr. Lying on the floor, in various conditions from collectable to rubbish, were dozens of cards most of which had gone out of production more than half a century before the works closed. Indeed, some of the examples dated from the very earliest years of the photographic postcard. They had been discarded when the cupboards in which they had been forgotten were sold.

The sheer number of cards relating to the mining industry which were produced in Wigan alone runs to many dozens, and coalfields around the country were celebrated in several hundred more. What is perhaps most surprising is that after so long, I am still coming across new finds – cards which have also hitherto escaped the notice of my collector friends.

Just about every aspect of the life, work and death of Edwardian miners was celebrated or commemorated in postcards, as well as detailed views of the collieries and the ancillary industries upon which they were dependent. What started out as a simple communication medium very quickly became an important, if accidental, means of chronicling Edwardian life.

The picture postcard was in its heyday in the Edwardian era and during the years leading up to the First World War. Just how many different mining-related cards were produced, we will never know, but this book stands as a celebration of the photographers and publishers whose postcards immortalised some of the hundreds of thousands of men and women who worked in the coal industry during the Edwardian years.

Very special thanks to Bob Allard, Mark Fynn, Richard Higgs, Marilyn and David Parkinson who have loaned me so many superb cards from their own collections, and as always, to my wife, Kath, for her constant support and encouragement.

John Hannavy, 2013

Opposite: Sarah Magin – known as Sal Madge – was born in a Penrith workhouse in 1831 and was already employed at Saltom Colliery, Westmorland, by the age of 8. She was one of thousands of children who worked underground until the practice was outlawed in 1842. A tall women who was often mistaken for a man – and thus one of the many 'curiosities' made famous by photography – Sal died in 1899. Cabinet photographs of her from the late 1880s, when she still worked as a pit brow lass, were published as tinted postcards a few years after her death.

PUBLISHING EDWARDIAN MINING POSTCARDS

Below. One of Warner Gothard's photo-montages of the explosion at Abram's Maypole Colliery in 1908.

IT WOULD BE hard to overstate the importance of the picture postcard in the daily lives of our Edwardian ancestors. In some respects a hundred years does not seem all that long a time – yet in other ways the lifestyle of people living at the beginning of the last century is so far removed from that which we experience today as to be almost unimaginable. That is what gives postcards their nostalgic appeal – the huge variety of photographs they carry are a unique record of past eras, and the messages written on the backs of them are what makes them an invaluable part of social history.

A century ago, in the days before every home had a telephone, and at a time when the post office collected and delivered mail several times a day, the picture postcard was the equivalent of today's text message – the quickest and most reliable way of making arrangements, contacting a friend, or offering best wishes for birthdays, anniversaries and

weddings, in the days before the widespread popularity of greetings cards.

Postcards mailed at 10am often carried the simple message "See you tonight at 7" or similar. At a halfpenny for a simple black and white card – and often as little as an old penny for a coloured view – and a halfpenny to post it, the postcard was the communication medium for everyman.

So popular did the postcard become – and so quickly – that in October 1903, a writer for the *Glasgow Evening News* predicted that "In ten years Europe will be buried beneath picture postcards". That was long before the photographic postcard had really become popular.

Below: Bamforth's early 1910 series *Heroes of the Mine*, used a view thought to be the Hulton Colliery's Pretoria Pit at Westhoughton Lancashire where an explosion later that year would cost 44 lives. The fourth card included an inset portrait of King Edward VII (see p.76).

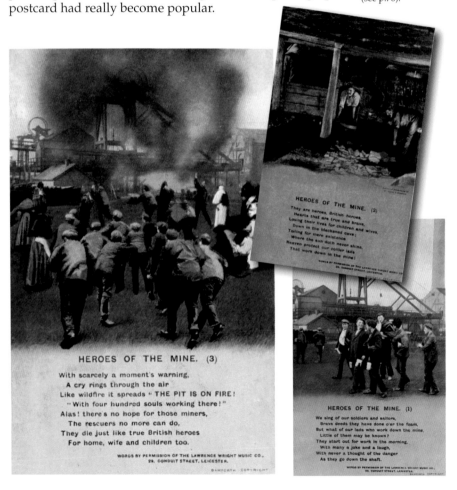

HEROES OF THE MINE. (3)

With scarcely a moment's warning,
  A cry rings through the air
Like wildfire it spreads " THE PIT IS ON FIRE!
  " With four hundred souls working there!"
Alas! there s no hope for those miners,
  The rescuers no more can do,
They die just like true British heroes
  For home, wife and children too.

WORDS BY PERMISSION OF THE LAWRENCE WRIGHT MUSIC CO.,
29, CONDUIT STREET, LEICESTER.

BAMFORTH COPYRIGHT.

HEROES OF THE MINE. (2)

They are heroes, British heroes,
  Hearts that are true and brave,
Losing their lives for children and wives,
  Down in the blackened cave;
Toiling for mere existence
  Where the sun doth never shine,
Heaven protect our collier lads
  That work down in the mine!

WORDS BY PERMISSION OF THE LAWRENCE WRIGHT MUSIC CO.,
29, CONDUIT STREET, LEICESTER.

HEROES OF THE MINE. (1)

We sing of our soldiers and sailors,
  Brave deeds they have done o'er the foam,
But what of our lads who work down the mine,
  Little of them may be known?
They start out for work in the morning,
  With many a joke and a laugh,
With never a thought of the danger
  As they go down the shaft.

WORDS BY PERMISSION OF THE LAWRENCE WRIGHT MUSIC CO.,
29, CONDUIT STREET, LEICESTER.

Several of the early colliery postcards were based on Thomas Taylor's photographs taken some years earlier. The postcard, below, published by James Starr, used a photograph taken at Pemberton Colliery in the late 1890s. The man in view was identified on the original photograph as Mr John Ritson, under-manager at the mine. The tinted postcard, c.1906, intended for national sale, does not identify the mine.

Although the picture postcard was only in its infancy at that time, the range of cards available during the Edwardian years was such that collecting was already a popular hobby.

There was already a magazine for collectors, *The Picture Postcard Magazine*, and in the same year its editor expressed amazement at the sales figures already being reported.

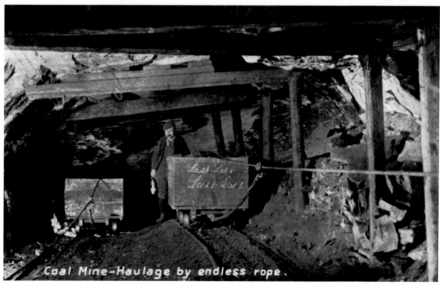

Coal Mine-Haulage by endless rope.

Rival companies vied with each other to produce the most popular card at any location. In addition to the expected range of scenic cards – and a vastly wider range than any town or city can offer today – every stationer sold humorous postcards, romantic ones, cards which told stories, included the words of songs, and dozens of other varieties.

James Starr re-published the central part of Taylor's photograph c.1908, this time within an elaborate 'lace' motif frame.

Some of the best tinted cards were produced in Saxony and Bavaria, where colour lithographic printing was of a much higher standard and a much lower cost than could be found in most British printing establishments. German cards were, therefore, widely considered to be 'quality' items!

All that changed with the advent of the Great War, of course. For the duration of the war, the purchase of remaining stock of pre-1914 cards which bore the legend 'Printed in Bavaria' or 'Printed at our Works in Saxony' was positively frowned upon as being unpatriotic – with these beautiful cards going from 'must have' to 'must not have' almost overnight!

As the pre-production costs were higher, tinted cards had to be produced in larger numbers to make economic sense for the publishers. But clearly the extra expense was rewarded with increased sales. Indeed so popular were some cards that publishers produced them in a range of different styles.

Coal Mine—Haulage by Endless Rope.

The simple black and white, or sepia cards of the early Edwardian years were sometimes republished tinted by the middle of the decade, and republished again with more elaborate framing and styling before the decade's end. That clearly points towards very successful marketing, even for relatively small publishers like James Starr of Wigan.

There are no reliable figures about just how many postcards were mailed annually in Britain in the early years

Cross, Tetley & Co.'s Bamfurlong Colliery – a Will Smith postcard c.1905, from a photograph by Thomas Taylor.

Left: French cards showed more of the non-mining activities in the colliery – such as the banks of furnaces which powered the steam engines.

Opposite page: Pemberton Collieries pit lasses, photographed c.1904.

Breaker Boys at Work by Raphael Tuck, c.1904, The caption reads "The first task of the little fellow who enters the mine is that of a breaker boy. In the dark and dusty screen room he sits on a hard bench built across a long chute, through which passed a steady stream of broken coal, and from which he picks out the piece of slate or rock."

of the last century, but estimates put the figure at 500 million. In stark contrast to the bland postcards generally available today, the Edwardians could choose from a varied and interesting range of lively and contemporary cards in just about every town and village.

Of course, there were many bland ones as well but, as the decade progressed and the range of cards was expanded, there was sufficient choice to ensure that if someone was contacting a friend several times a month, then the chances of duplicating a card could be minimised!

The rise of the picture postcard brought with it many cultural changes. Not long after the earliest postcards appeared, their status was the subject of some dire warnings to anyone concerned with 'doing the right thing'. When the 1894 edition of Oliver Bunce's essential guide *Don't: A manual of mistakes and improprieties* was published, the author advised his readers that they should not "conduct correspondence on postal cards. It is questionable whether a note on a postal card is entitled to the courtesy of a response."

This photograph taken by Thomas Taylor underground at Blundell's Pemberton Colliery in 1898 – the date is chalked on the coal face behind the miners – was used six years later by James Starr for the postcard, below, titled 'Coal Mine – testing the roof'. The date is written in chalk on the coal face itself. Taking photographs underground at that time posed significant risks – early flash powder would have been too hazardous to be used in mines where firedamp was always present, so some early electric lighting must have been employed.

Of course, as postcard usage mushroomed into the Edwardian era, the humble card was almost always used to carry a message which did not require the immediate courtesy of a reply, and in that respect, Bunce's warning proved unnecessary.

The postcard would turn out to be a device seldom used for correspondence as a two-way activity, but more often for the quite new phenomenon of simply saying 'wish you were here'.

The 'standard size' picture postcard – 5½" x 3½" – was agreed by the International Postal Union on 1 September 1899,

13

Above: For this postcard of the victims of the disaster at Norton Hill Colliery, Midsomer Norton, in the Somerset coalfield, the Gothards used photographs taken by F. G. Steggles whose studio was in Shepton Mallet.

Right: From around the same time, a view of the colliery at work, with railway wagons being loaded from the coal chutes.

just over five years after postal regulations had been changed to allow privately printed cards to be sent through the post. That size was actually the maximum permitted under the new legislation. 'Court Cards', measuring 4½" x 3½" had by then been in production for nearly thirty years, although prior to 1894 they had had to be enclosed in an envelope before posting.

The first postcards, as might be expected, were scenics, and George Stewart of Edinburgh and Raphael Tuck of London have claims to be amongst the earliest if not the first.

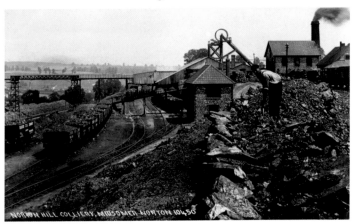

Photographic postcards appeared before the end of the nine-teenth century, and 'real photograph' cards by 1900. Frederick Corkett of the British Photographic publishing Company of Leicester introduced his first photographic cards in 1899, but was working for Tuck by 1900.

Pickers getting coal from the Waste Dump – an American postcard mailed in 1910, publisher unknown. Picking coal from spoil heaps was a universal practice to which colliery owners across the world usually turned a blind eye. For such a subject to have been used as a postcard, they would certainly have had to!

The coal industry was just one of many subjects to attract the interest of the postcard publishers, but it is unclear just when the first mining card went on sale in Britain. The oldest which has been confirmed during the research undertaken for this book dates from 1903 or 1904, although the original photographs used as the basis of some of the earliest tinted cards date from the 1890s.

It was not just in Britain that the subject proved to have considerable appeal with the public – mining postcards were produced in significant numbers in France, Belgium, Germany and, of course, the United States. While Europe concentrated on extensive series of monochrome cards – often including a verse of poetry written by a miner – in Britain and America the tinted postcard proved the most popular. Views of collieries, groups of miners, pit girls, and the various stages of the mining operation all featured on cards. In France, the subject matter was broadened to include the men who stoked the boilers which powered the mine, and detailed views of the equipment.

Below: Entitled
'Peebles Worthies'
this postcard was
mailed to a collector
in New South Wales
in September 1906.
The message simply
reads "Geordie
and Kirsty, coal
carriers. Kirsty died
a fortnight ago,
11-9-06." Through
postcards, these
hard-working casual
workers became
local celebrities

Opposite: Two
postcards of
'Petticoat Dan' of
Kirkintilloch.

The Wigan Pit Brow Lasses had been famous since the 1860s and the carte-de-visite collecting craze, so the postcard publishers knew there would be a ready market for portraits of them, singly and in groups, in monochrome and on tinted cards.

Women working in the French and Belgian coalfields, known as Trieuses – coal-sorters or graders – were equally popular subjects, although rarely printed in colour.

Less famous – and certainly less celebrated in cards – were their male counterparts, the Breaker Boys who broke up and graded anthracite, and removed stone from the screens.

Boys over the age of twelve, once a common sight in Welsh pit yards, were still employed in the coalfields of Pennsylvania until well after the Great War. Too young to go underground, this gruelling work was a hard apprenticeship for a lifetime working in the mines.

While the majority of cards were produced locally, national publishers including Raphael Tuck and Francis Frith, marketed series of cards. Amongst the subjects featured, postcards were used to commemorate local tragedies. Disaster postcards were quite common – often sold to raise small sums of money for the victims, but others simply because the pictures were

newsworthy and likely to arouse public interest.

Celebrating the coal industry in postcards, however, often extended well beyond the pit gates.

Postcards showed coal merchants delivering coal, and perhaps more unusually, the local 'characters' who fulfilled their own small but important role in the whole process.

Edwardian coal merchants usually only delivered the coal as far as the front gate, or the foot of the tenement stairs, and it was up to the owner or tenant to arrange delivery to the actual house.

That is where people like 'Petticoat Dan' came into the picture. Visitors to Kirkintilloch in Scotland could purchase several postcards of this local character. Dan Cooper, who wore a skirt all his life, found regular employment shovelling coal for the townsfolk, and established a virtual monopoly, subjecting rivals to notorious tirades of abuse!

His obituary in the *Kirkintilloch Herald* in February 1913 observed that

> *A visit to Kirkintilloch by an outsider was always memorable if perchance Dan was met on the street, and many who have visited the town by the Queen steamers remember Kirkintilloch by little else.*

Writing to Master Henry Drabble in Derby in 1909, using a postcard of Dan with his mighty shovel, Henry's mother wrote "This is a man who has never had any trousers on, and as you can see he is an old man now, but poor chap, Dan is not as bright as he might be."

Dan died in 1913 at the age of 78. In his long life, the furthest he had ever travelled was the few miles to Glasgow – once! An orphan from a very early age, he was given a small weekly allowance by the Parish Council, who also, perhaps somewhat surprisingly, provided his clothes!

In several towns, perhaps for a few pennies, local worthies and eccentrics were persuaded into the photographer's studio to be similarly immortalised on postcards.

Sometimes the message on the back of a postcard bore no relationship whatsoever to the photograph on the front – the message had an immediate and short-lived relevance; the card itself might be treasured and added to

Amongst the many cards produced to illustrate and commemorate the Maypole disaster near Wigan, this composite card was produced by letter-press printing and published by the Economic Printing Co., of Pershore Road in Birmingham. It claims 72 dead, not 75.

Below: Seven members of Lancashire's Howe Bridge Rescue Team pose with their new breathing apparatus, published as a postcard between 1908 and 1910.

the recipient's growing collection. Some highly incongruous pairings have survived.

"Dear Aunt", wrote Len from Walsall to Mrs H. Dixon of Oldbury, Worcestershire on a card posted at 3.45pm on eighteenth March 1908, "Will you please come on Wednesday for rug. If not convenient then tomorrow Tuesday will do". The card he used was, perhaps surprisingly, a photo-montage

18

Lump of Coal weighing 15 tons.

This 15 ton block of coal was brought out of the Yard Level of the Tredegar Iron Company's mine in South Wales in 1851. Originally cut at 20 tons – the largest piece of coal ever to be brought out of a British mine – a 5 ton piece fell off while it was being loaded on to a railway trick. It was intended to be the centrepiece of the company's display at the Great Exhibition, but it proved impossible to transport it to London. The block was moved to Bedwelty Park in Tredegar where it remains on display to this day.

published by Warner Gothard of Barnsley of the disastrous fire which had swept through the Hamstead Colliery at Great Barr, Birmingham, just two weeks earlier on 4 March. A simple message about a rug on one side; and on the other, the story of the deaths of 25 miners and one rescuer, and the successful rescue of six more.

Even stranger was the decision of toy shop owners Hamel-Jallier & Cie, of 7 Rue de la Paix in Laval , France, when selecting a postcard to advertise their Christmas gift range in 1906. Their bizarre choice of card was a photograph of one of the funeral processions in the aftermath of Europe's worst mining disaster

Dover Colliery seen from Shakespeare Cliffs in a postcard c.1904. From the outset in 1896, the colliery was beset by problems of roof collapses and flooding, and by the time the project was abandoned ten years later, not a single ton of coal had ever been mined.

Aberaman Colliery in the Cynon Valley in South Wales, opened in 1840, the shaft descending to a depth of 250ft. By the early 1900s, 1,739 miners were working the 'Lower Four Feet' seam 800ft underground. This postcard dates from c.1909 and was sent by Harry Smart who was 'trying to get down the bottom'.

Below: Although this card was posted in Northumberland, the mine and miners shown in this scene, titled 'Lunch Hour, a Typical Mining Scene' published by the Souvenir Post Card Company c.1910, are probably American.

which had taken place at Courrières on 10 March that year, and in which 1099 men and boys had died!

Perhaps buying the card in bulk increased the widows' fund, for most of the profits from such cards usually went to a fund for the widows and dependents. With such a huge death toll, funds from any source would have been essential. In the years before newspapers were regularly illustrated with photographs, postcard publishers were often the first to

publish visual accounts of the great events of the day. Disasters of all sort were obvious subjects for such cards.

Warner Gothard's sons developed the commemorative photo-montage postcard, probably drawing on their existing experience as photographers. Warner himself had been a professional photographer since the early 1850s, so was probably already well-versed in the technical intricacies of the photo-montage.

Producing photo-montage cartes-de-visite and cabinet prints had long been a common practice amongst photographers,

Above: Policemen pose for the camera after the 1910 riots at the Powell Duffryn Colliery Company's Aberaman pit. Sixty people were injured

Below: 'A glimpse of child labor' wrote Aida Sherman from Nicholson, Pennsylvania to her friend Estelle Pittman in Hamilton, Ohio, in 1910. 'These are the breaker boys who pick the slate and stone out of the coal as it is sent down the chutes in the Breaker.' At the time this postcard was published, there were still more than 24,000 children employed in this work in American collieries, and the practice continued until the early 1920s.

involving the creation of large painted background artwork, on which were pasted the component images, the whole then being re-photographed. It is likely a similar technique was adapted for the production of these postcards. Warner Junior, and his brother Joseph, are generally credited with the creation of the company's first montaged card, commemorating a railway accident in which seven died which took place on 19 January 1905 on the Midland Railway near Cudworth, just a few miles from Gothard's studio in Barnsley. The two identified cards showing the wreckage are credited to Gothard of Leeds and Barnsley.

Over the following dozen years, the studio would produce cards commemorating some of the major national catastrophes – travelling far afield to cover some of them – the level of sophistication of their cards rising all the while.

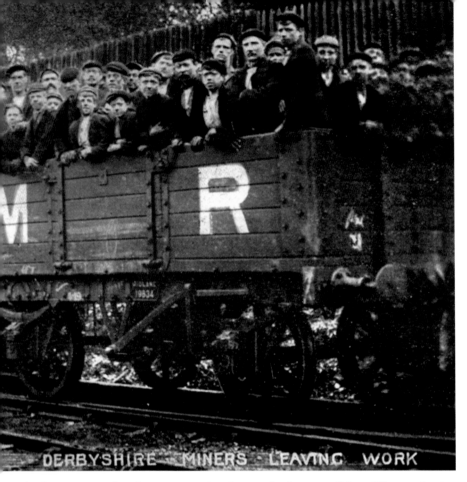

DERBYSHIRE MINERS LEAVING WORK

As far as researches have ascertained, a total of seven of the country's many Edwardian mining disasters featured in their catalogue. The first two were close to home – at Barnsley's Barrow Colliery, where seven men died on 15 November 1907, and Hoyland Silkstone Colliery, only a few miles away just eight days later, where a boiler explosion cost four lives. Travelling to those from their Elsdon Street studio in Barnsley would have been easy.

That second accident resulted in a poignant mention in the *London Gazette* of 18 January 1908 –

The King has been pleased to award the Edward Medal of the First Class to Mr. Francis Chandler for his great bravery in saving life in a disaster which took place at the Hoyland Silk-stone Colliery, on the 23rd November last. Chandler, who is

This unusual post-card produced as part of the 'Peverill Series' shows a trainload of miners on their way home from Shipley Colliery c.1907. Was some local hierarchy at work here which dictated who travelled in the carriages and who had to settle for the open coal trucks?

sixty years of age, was engaged with five others in repairing an underground boiler house, when a fall of roof took place which broke an iron girder and damaged the boiler, from which a rush of steam took place. All the men were scalded and hurt; one was killed on the spot and three others died afterwards. The lamps were extinguished. Although badly burnt and hurt, Chandler crept in the dark three times through the steam to the boiler top, to rescue others who could not move, at the risk of his own life. Being then unable to do more alone, he signalled to the pit top and was drawn up. Although almost exhausted he insisted on again descending the pit to assist in the rescue. His son was one of the victims of the disaster.

Two Wigan Pit Brow Lasses wearing breeches pose for the camera for one of the extensive 'Wrench Series' postcards, published around 1904.

The other accidents featured by Gothard were those at the Glebe Colliery, County Durham, 20 February 1908; Hamstead Colliery, Great Barr, 4 March 1908; Midsomer Norton, 9 April 1908; the Maypole disaster near Wigan, 18 August 1908, and the West Stanley explosion 16 February 1909. Examples from all of those are illustrated later in this book.

Postcards of two other disasters – at Wharncliffe Silkstone Colliery Barnsley on 30 May 1914, and Halmerend in Staffordshire on 17 January 1915, were also published by the company.

Other publishers also produced photo-composites, but they rarely matched the quality of the Gothard cards. Invariably printed by either lithography or poor quality letterpress printing, such cards lacked the apparent authority and authenticity of Gothard's real photographic prints. The machine-printed cards were probably produced in greater numbers, but were also certainly less collectable.

Colliery Lasses.

The Wrench Series.   No. 3722

24

German coal miners in their 'dress uniforms' preparing to take part in a parade. Taken in Frieberg, and published as an undivided back postcard c.1905.

Every Gothard card was an original photographic print hand-made in their darkrooms, the clarity of the portraits of the victims was much higher than cards produced by letterpress or lithograhpy, and a share of the profits from most of the Gothard cards went into funds to benefit the widows and children of the lost miners.

Not all composite cards were factually based. Bamforths of Holmfirth in Yorkshire pioneered composites illustrating the songs and hymns of the day – amongst them several cards featuring the perils of mining.

Joseph Bamforth had started producing lantern slides to do the same job as early as the 1870s. For lantern slide shows in local halls and working men's clubs, Bamforth's slides contained the words of popular songs and hymns, illustrated with carefully constructed photographic images, often made up from several different pictures, and then laboriously tinted by hand. For the original photographs, he would first produce a careful sketch of exactly where every element within the picture should be, and then careful pose models and props to recreate the desired scene. His son, Edwin, saw the potential of applying his father's techniques to the production of postcards, and Bamforths 'Song Cards' started to appear c.1904. Several of them are illustrated in this book.

Edwardian plate cameras were large and cumbersome, and difficult to manipulate and focus in the confined spaces and low light levels underground.

70/-

Cylar's
'Populi'
Half-plate
Outfit

Fig. 6.

25

Perhaps conscious of the need to produce pleasing – and wherever possible picturesque – views, and aware of the fact that featuring expanses of despoiled land would counter that endeavour, only a few of the publishers who produced postcards of collieries ever included spoil heaps in their photographs, most seeking to portray the image of a well organised and carefully managed industry.

Exceptions to that would be the cards showing coal-pickers scavanging for fuel on the tips – a few of which were published before 1910, and several more during the pre-First World War miners' strikes.

Indeed, the height of the spoil heap often gave photographers a very good viewpoint from which to take their photographs, looking down on the more orderly and organised expanse of the pit yard and associated railway sidings.

The steep hillsides surrounding South Wales collieries nestling in narrow valleys also gave the photographers great vantage points from which to take their pictures.

Underground, for the postcard photographers, the challenges were much greater – working in cramped conditions with large cameras and primitive lighting, their skills were tested to the limit. There were three forms of artificial light in use by photographers at the time – acetylene, flash powder or ribbon, and electric light. As acetylene involved igniting a highly flammable gas, and open flash utilised a burning magnesium ribbon, neither was a safe option in mines, especially coal mines where there was a risk of gas. That left only electric lamps as the safe option but, in the Edwardian years, early incandescent bulbs also produced the least intense light.

Indeed, the first photographs produced using magnesium as the light source can probably be traced back to 1867 when American Civil War photographer Timothy O'Sullivan photographed in the gold and silver mines of Nevada – but there was no risk of igniting pockets of gas in such mines.

Opposite page: Sarah Leech, aged eight years, and Jack Bowker, aged five disappeared at three o'clock in the afternoon of Sunday, 27 February, 1910 while out playing in a field a few yards from their homes. The cap on a disused and long-forgotten pit shaft from the Glass House Fold Colliery had suddenly given way beneath their feet. They were not discovered until half-past eight next morning – for sixteen and a half hours they had been trapped at the bottom of the pitshaft. After briefly crying, they wrapped themselves in Jack's jacket and slept, waking only when they heard helpers up above! They were hauled to the surface one at a time in a basket.

Left: Detail from a postcard c.1902, entitled 'A scene on Cannock Chase', showing the 2ft gauge 0-4-0ST locomotive *Colonel Wilson*, built in 1897 by Manning Wardle & Co. Ltd., Leeds, Works No. 1371.

Left: Many colliery companies had interests in iron and steel works. Wigan Coal & Iron Company's Kirkless Ironworks was one of the largest.

In British tin mines, the use of the intense light generated by flash produced some remarkable 'instantaneous' images, but in collieries, many of which suffered from firedamp, the risks were considered unacceptably high, and the use of open flash lights or flares had been banned in coal mines by the 1870s. As flash powder or ribbon gave off clouds of dense white smoke after the flash burned out, its use in any case would render further mining in the immediate vicinity quite impossible for some time after the photograph was taken!

All Edwardian underground coal mining pictures, therefore, were taken using electric light and, as exposure times were of several seconds' duration even with the most sensitive glass plates then available, all were dependent on the active participation of the miners. The men all had to be posed, and they had to hold their position for three or more seconds. That the resulting pictures look so natural is a testament to the skill of the photographers and the willing compliance of the miners. Every underground photograph. therefore, was the result of very careful planning, and involved the transportation underground of a great deal of bulky equipment.

This view of miners during their lunch break underground in a gold mine at Cripple Creek, Colorado, was published as a postcard in 1908.

The usual size of photographic plate used by photographers at the turn of the century was either 'half plate' (6½ x 4½ ins) or 'whole plate' (6½ x 8½ ins), the former being the one most ideally suited to being cropped down to the standard postcard size of 5½ x 3½ ins.

Such cameras were relatively large. In addition, the photographer would have carried several 'darkslides' each holding two photographic plates, a sturdy tripod on which to mount the camera, three or four electric lamps, an assortment of cables, and large battery cells to power the lights. Existing underground lighting would not have proved sufficient.

Film cameras taking postcard-size negatives, most notably the Kodak No. 3A and 3B folding cameras were introduced in 1903, and were sold until 1915, enabling amateurs to produce their own postcards. These cameras, however, were rarely used by professionals.

But, of course, it was not just coal mining which caught the public's imagination. The men who dug for tin, gold, silver and a host of other minerals were also celebrated in series of postcards across the world. Publishers featured the gold

Chinese labourers were introduced into the Transvaal goldfield in 1904, to compensate for a labour shortage after the Boer Wars, and by 1908 there were more than 100,000 of them employed in the mines.

Chinese Mining Boys

1186 Published by Sallo Epstein & Co., Durban

miners of America, Australia and South Africa, the Canadian silver miners, and the Cornish tin and copper miners, as well as views of salt mines, lead mines and slate quarries.

What marks all these cards out is their focus on people rather than just places. We are invited to look briefly into the lives of these early miners, their workplaces, their families, and the hardships and dangers which they faced.

For the postcard publishers, however, their interest did not stop at the pit gates. They were keen to cover every aspect of the industry, and that included everything from domestic coal merchants through to the great coal docks which dominated many British ports and, of course, the coaling towers which delivered fuel deep into the bowels of steamships.

Postcards thus tell the whole story of the mining industry, from the sinking of the shafts through the transport, export and delivery of the coal, up to and including the funerals of those who paid with their lives to produce that coal.

No other Edwardian industry was celebrated as comprehensively and engagingly on the humble postcard as mining was, and probably only a very few aspects of a collier's life and work were overlooked. And even unfortunate accidents which came about as a result of mining were commemorated in short-run and locally produced cards.

Above: The Camborne & Redruth Tramway, seen here in a pre-1910 postcard, was used to carry ore from the Camborne tin mines. It opened in 1902, and survived until 1934.

Opposite: A 'Peacock Series' postcard from c.1907, titled 'Miners Descending Pit near Redruth'. Redruth was the centre of the tin and copper mining industry, with several mines in the immediate vicinity. The location of this card is probably East Pool Mine, the subject of an extensive series of coloured postcards.

The coal dock at Methil in Fife. This small port exported over a million tons of coal from the Fife coalfields each year.

Refuelling a steamer at the coaling towers in Barry Docks, South Wales, 1903.

Below: Detail from a late Edwardian postcard showing the coal tips at Penarth Docks.

After all, sending a postcard with a picture on it of someone you know – or knew – must have been quite an added attraction.

Mining even featured in the hugely popular 'Song Cards' produced by Bamforth & Company of Holmfirth in Yorkshire, the first of which appeared in 1910. Four series of cards with a mining theme are known to have been produced. This chapter opened with *Heroes of the Mine*, and the most famous of them, *Don't Go Down in the Mine, Dad*, is discussed later in this book.

Above: Millions of tons of coal from the Durham coalfield were shipped from the Lambton Coal Drops in Sunderland Docks, seen here c.1910.

Left: Coal boats delivering domestic supplies to Padstow, Cornwall c.1902.

The series *A Miner's Dream of Home,* which was first published in 1913, chimed with the Edwardian love of a good melodrama, while *The Collier's Life*, illustrated on these pages, was published in 1912 as "A Memento of the Great Colliery Strike". With its strong political message – "And think of the widows when paying a wage, And a pension to them be allowed" – campaigning for pension rights for miners and, more importantly for their widows was gaining pace at the time. It was, without doubt, the most poignant of the song card series, given the considerable hardships suffered in the mining industry at the time.

The quality of the printing and production of all the early tinted mining cards suggests that high volume sales were

Above: Slide 15 from the Bamforth 18-lantern slide series *The Collier's Life* is the only surviving example yet discovered. It would be projected to illustrate the line 'Next morning at daybreak, he stood by the pit, Midst agonised children and wives'. The company also produced a 20-slide series for *Don't go Down in the Mine, Dad* and a series of slides to illustrate *Heroes of the Mine*. They are all extremely rare today. All the images, for song cards or lantern slides, were staged using actors, often photographed in real colliery locations.

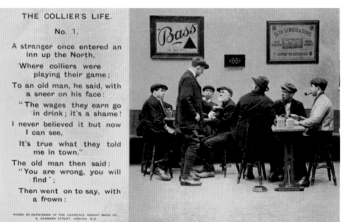

THE COLLIER'S LIFE.

No. 1.

A stranger once entered an
  inn up the North,
Where colliers were
  playing their game;
To an old man, he said, with
  a sneer on his face:
"The wages they earn go
  in drink; it's a shame!
I never believed it but now
  I can see,
It's true what they told
  me in town."
The old man then said:
"You are wrong, you will
  find";
Then went on to say, with
  a frown:

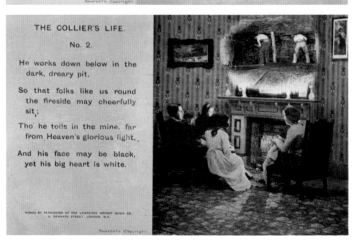

THE COLLIER'S LIFE.

No. 2.

He works down below in the
  dark, dreary pit,

So that folks like us round
  the fireside may cheerfully
  sit;

Tho' he toils in the mine, far
  from Heaven's glorious light,

And his face may be black,
  yet his big heart is white.

THE COLLIER'S LIFE.

No. 3.

The stranger, ashamed, at
once turned from the inn,
When outside a cry rent
the air :
" The pit is on fire and the
night shift's below !"
He flew to the pit shaft,
but ere he' got there,
The lads from yon brightly
lit room had arrived,
All eager to go down
below.
The stranger, amazed, to
himself he then said :
"Ah! the miner I'm
getting to know."

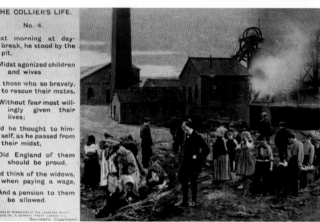

THE COLLIER'S LIFE.

No. 4.

Next morning at day-
break, he stood by the
pit,
'Midst agonized children
and wives
Of those who so bravely,
to rescue their mates,
Without fear most will-
ingly given their
lives;
And he thought to him-
self, as he passed from
their midst,
Old England of them
should be proud,
And think of the widows,
when paying a wage,
And a pension to them
be allowed.

The sheet music for
The Collier's Life,
with words by
Eltham Green and
music by M. Nagle,
was published by
Lawrence Wright
Music in 1912, at the
time of the miners'
strike – a strike
which had been the
logical conclusion of
the unrest which
had been simmering
since 1909, and
which had shut all
the country's mines
down for five weeks.
Bamforth's four
postcards of the
song appeared
shortly afterwards,
together with an
18-slide set of
lantern slides.

expected and achieved – a great number of them destined never
to be sent through the post, but rather to be preserved in
growing postcard collections across the world – postcard
collecting as a hobby is almost as old as the postcard itself, and
certainly pre-dates the photographic card by some years.

Local published 'real photograph' cards were obviously
produced in much smaller numbers, their sales restricted to
those who had a direct involvement with the scenes thus
depicted. That scarcity, and the very local events which they
commemorate, increases their appeal to collectors today.

Thanks to their careful preservation for over a hundred years
now, all these postcards offer us a fascinating insight into
Edwardian social history.

DIGGING FOR BLACK DIAMONDS

Opposite, top:
Dinner time for the
evicted children at
the 'Kinsley Hotel'.

Opposite, below:
The eviction camp
with, in the distance,
the recently made
tents.

Below: Bretby
Colliery's prize
pony, a postcard by
J. S. Simnett, Burton-
on-Trent.

BRETBY COLLIERY in Derbyshire was, a century ago, one of many which employed ponies underground. Their handlers were well aware of the value of fresh air, and from time to time, the ponies were brought to the surface and given a few weeks off from their heavy work at the pit bottom.

Perhaps surprisingly, after spending weeks on end below ground – they were usually stabled near the bottom of the shaft as well – the ponies' eyesight quickly adjusted to the brightness, and they enjoyed their brief 'freedom' in lush pasture. In a rare postcard, a boy stands proudly alongside 'Skye', one of Bretby's ponies which had, on 4 September 1907, just been awarded first prize at Ashby-de-la-Zouch Agricultural Show. Behind the pony and the boy, the winding gear of the colliery's two shafts can be seen.

Today, of course, the colliery has gone, and the village's only connection with mining is the presence of one of British Coal's research centres in the local business park.

1ST PRIZE PIT PONY. "SKYE" FROM BRETBY COLLIERY ASHBY-DE-LA ZOUCH A. S. SHOW SEPT 4TH 1907.

Evicted Children's Quarters
dinner time at Kinsley Hotel SEP 11/05
Photo by Wales, Hemsworth

The speed with which all but a few traces of Britain's mining industry have disappeared has been remarkable. Derelict pit yards have been landscaped and turned into country parks, industrial estates and shopping centres; spoil heaps have been removed and used as bottoming for motorways. But the mining

WA. "EVICTED CAMP" OF HEMSWORTH MINERS. AUG 1905

Kinsley Evictions
Oct 3|05
Photo by Wales

Evicting two policemen.

Despite the bitterness of the evictions, everyone on this postcard appears surprisingly good-humoured.

industry was about so much more than just mines and annual tallies of coal production. Mining villages were, primarily, about people, about shared lives, shared risks, and all too often shared deaths. It has been said of many mining communities that when there was a roof fall, or an explosion, in which lives were lost, the sense of shared loss was palpable.

What has been swept away was more than just places of work – collieries were at the heart of so many communities, all of them close-knit, all of them proudly independent yet fiercely loyal to each other.

In Edwardian times, miners invariably lived in tied cottages, and spent their earnings in shops owned and operated by their employers. Thus, disputes became major issues – standing against the colliery owner could cost not just a miner's job, but his home as well.

Kinsley Hemsworth Colliery in Yorkshire was one of several where a dispute in 1905 escalated to the point where the owner literally turned the miners' families out on to the street, requiring them to seek temporary accommodation in church halls, and a tented camp a short distance from their village.

A local photographer identified only as 'Wales' captured the story, and produced a series of highly journalistic

Left and below: The Kinsley postcards ably demonstrate the strong sense of community which existed in mining areas.

postcards. He photographed everything from the actual evictions, the tented camp which was set up, the communal kitchens, the special care of the miners' children, and even miners and other local workmen getting together to make the tents. His postcards depict a community the members of which which drew strength from supporting each other and, in times of crisis, pooled their resources and expertise in support of the common cause – a feature of mining communities across the country and across the centuries.

Since the 1970s, not only have most mines closed, but even the last remaining traces of them have been erased from the landscape.

Above: Tent making for the evicted Kinsley Hemsworth Miners, August 1905.

Many communities have been torn apart by the demise of the coal industry and the acrimony surrounding its collapse. Tens of thousands of miners, thrown out of work when their pits closed, continue daily to suffer the ravages which a lifetime of coal dust have wrought on their lungs. Yet, many

still yearn for a job which employed generation after generation; where son followed father below ground, and where there was a comradeship born out of shared risk.

That comradeship, that pride in the work, shines out from the legacy of photographs which tell the visual history of coal mining. Edwardian miners – shoulders back, chests out, picks in hand – posed proudly for the many postcard publishers who would immortalise them. There is an intimate quality to the locally-produced photo-cards which the mass-produced national published cards never equalled.

The nineteenth century had seen a huge increase in demand for coal, as Britain's industries became increasingly mechanised, as the number and size of ships grew exponentially, and as the railways spread their way across the country. The sheer number of people employed in the industry which met that demand also constituted a huge potential postcard market in itself

The development of steam power not only increased demand for coal, it also made possible the extraction of coal from deeper and more difficult underground environments.

Steam powered the pumps which kept mines drained; steam powered the bellows which increased the flow of fresh air hundreds and later thousands of feet underground; steam

Above: 'Miners leaving the Pit', a view of an unidentified Lancashire colliery, probably Bamfurlong Mains, from a photograph c.1900, probably by Thomas Taylor, published as a James Starr postcard c.1905.

Opposite: The boiler house was at the heart of every coal mine, providing the power for the cages, the coal screens, and the air supply for the miners below ground. The furnaces burned unsaleable coal dross. This view is from the USA.

Above: 'At the Coal Level, Aberdare', from a photograph by Ray. This postcard was published c.1905.

Below: Ashington in Northumberland was known as 'the biggest mining village in the world', This view shows colliery's railway yards c.1904.

powered the winches which raised and lowered the cages taking the men to coalfaces at hitherto impossible depths, and brought the coal up to the surface. Almost one ton in forty of all the coal mined in Britain was, by the end of the century, being burned in vast arrays of Lancashire boilers to power the mines themselves. This was not the extravagance it might seem. Newcomen pumping engines, and most of the boilerhouses of Britain's mines, were fuelled with dross – effectively coal waste which could not easily be sold on the general market.

Thus, on colliery balance sheets, the fuel to power the equipment was, to all intents and purposes, a free by-product of the mining process itself.

According to official records, the total number of deep mines extracting coal in Britain a little over a century ago was 3236. They employed more than a million men and women – the men working below ground, the women in the pit yards, coal screens and washeries. Women and children had been banned from working underground in the 1840s.

The bottom of the pit shaft at Bamfurlong Colliery's No. 4 pit, photographed by Thomas Taylor of Platt Bridge, in 1889 and published as a postcard c.1904. This shaft gave access to the rich coal seam known as the 'Wigan six foot'.

Most of these collieries were operated by a number of privately-owned mining conglomerates, the remainder run by small independent colliery companies. Many of the smaller colliery companies worked either single deep pits or drift mines. Miners usually worked in small teams, even in the Edwardian era, and payment was usually based on the team's daily output.

The annual output from Britain's collieries in 1905, was a staggering 236 million tons. Of that, over 7 million tons was used by the collieries themselves to drive their machinery. By comparison, that latter figure is largely the same as the

Dinner time in a coalmine, a postcard using a photograph taken by J. A. Snape of Bridgtown, Cannock. Not postally used, and believed to be c.1910.

There was a colliery right underneath Bilton Town Hall, which featured in several postcards! This card showing coal being brought up from that seam under the town centre, was postally used on 23 May 1906. The photograph was taken by Bennett Clark of Wolverhampton – who operated his studio at 74 Darlington Street from 1888 until his death in 1937. It was published as a postcard by John Price and Sons of Market Place, Bilston.

current total output for UK Coal, Britain's last company operating deep mines, which in 2011 extracted just 7.5 million tons – a slight increase on 2010.

In the Edwardian era a further 8 million tons powered Britain's railways, 10 million tons was used to generate coal gas for street lighting and domestic lighting and cooking, and 21 million tons were burned in the country's household ranges and fireplaces. Those figures, however, pale into insignificance against the estimated 50 million tons which powered the factories and industrial complexes of Edwardian Britain.

Just like any other natural product, the coal which lay beneath the British landscape varied considerably in quality and therefore in application. Thus the output from different coalfields fed quite different markets.

The geology of coal is complex, and it was not unusual for seams at different levels in the same colliery to have significantly different combustion characteristics. Some might be best suited for use in railway locomotives and ships – steam coal – whilst a seam just a few hundred feet below might yield coal of a completely different nature, ideally suited for the domestic market.

In Victorian and Edwardian times, amongst the most sought after was 'navigation' or 'steam' coal – especially widespread in both the Welsh and Fife coalfields – which was

GETTING COAL IN THE MAIN STREET AT BILSTON

Miners cutting navigation coal in the Lochgelly Splint seam at Bowhill Colliery in Fife, from an extensive series of photographs taken underground in 1906, and later published as tinted postcards by Valentine. Several seams were worked in the pit: the Lochgelly Splint, at 1000 ft depth yielded good steam coal; the Lochgelly Parrott, gas coal; the Five Foot, 2nd class coal, and the Dunfermline Splint, best household. The seams varied in thickness between one and five feet.

ideally suited for burning in the furnaces of steam ships. Millions of tons of the stuff were burned each year and, in the Edwardian years, with huge expansion of both merchant and naval fleets, demand increased considerably year on year.

Navigation coal had especially attractive heat-producing properties derived from the fact that it combined a high proportion of carbon with a burning characteristic known as *cauliflowering* in the trade.

This meant that when it became hot, the coal developed pores through which the air draught could naturally migrate. Once it was lit, it burned steadily and highly efficiently, and this meant that steam could be generated, and steam pressure maintained, without the fire having to be poked or raked – and when dealing with a bank of several dozen steamship boilers in an already very hot boiler room, the less often the furnace doors had to be opened – apart from regular stoking – the more consistent the power output of the engines.

Coals with a low sulphur content were ideal for coking – effectively baking – to create the coke which burned with such intense heat that was ideal for blast furnaces. Poorest of the lot was 'brown coal' – a form of lignite – a dirty fuel which gave off a lot of smoke and a great deal of carbon dioxide – better known today as a primary 'greenhouse gas'. At the other end of the scale was cannel coal, or 'candle coal', a hydrogen-rich coal which burned with a bright flame, was easily lit, and left virtually no ash.

Another of the 1906 Bowhill series of views taken more than 1000ft underground, this one is titled 'Brushing the Roads'. In a colliery, the term 'roads' referred to the tunnel as a whole, and not just the railway track-bed. Here the roof appears to be supported by steel girders. Redundant sections of railway track were often used, rather than wooden props.

Below: 'A Good Shot', one of 24 cards produced c.1910 by Aspatria chemist John Pattinson. The series, taken in No. 4 Brayton Pit, and No. 5 Aspatria Pit, illustrate the whole production process.

It was so hard it could be turned, carved and polished to make beautiful ornaments. In the sixteenth century Wigan Cannel was found surprisingly close to the surface, in a seam which became known as the Great Haigh fault. The shallow depth of the seam meant that it was ideally suited to the simple surface mining methods available at that time. It could be worked and carved, and was an excellent light fuel.

Tradition has it than Wigan Cannell was so clean when polished, that you could eat food off plates made out of it

No. 5. A GOOD "SHOT."
Coal blasted down and ready for filling 350 yards below ground. Note the Shot Firer with battery and cable.
BRAYTON DOMAIN COLLIERIES   NO. 5 PIT, ASPATRIA

Another under-
ground view of 'The
brushers at work',
photographed in an
unidentified Scottish
coalmine, from the
'Scottish Coal Mine'
series, publisher
unknown, c.1910.

without fear of contamination, and according to folklore,
dinner plates have been made of the stuff and, after the meal
was over, been thrown in the fire to keep the dining room
warm! Certainly some beautifully made artifacts survive
made of the material.

Cannel was also found at varying depths in the Welsh and
Durham coalfields, as well as in the United States, and
because of the bright flame it could yield, the main use for
this hydrogen rich coal in the nineteenth century was in the
fuelling of gas lighting in the days before the invention of the
gas mantle.

A Lancashire Miner
at the coal face, one
of Wigan publisher
Will Smith's series of
mining postcards
c.1905.

In a Wigan trade directory from 1889, a one and a half page 'advertorial' was devoted to the operations of the Wigan Coal & Iron Company, at that time approaching its 25th anniversary.

The company was already experimenting with electric lighting below ground, and had long prided itself on the use of 'Muesler' safety lamps from Belgium, which were believed to offer a brighter and safer light than many others.

The Wigan Coal and Iron Company's coals are known in all parts of the United Kingdom and abroad, and have a high reputation wherever they have been used. The various pits supply different classes of coal, the variety being large enough to meet every requirement of the manufacturer, the gas company, and the householder. The gas and cannell coals of the company have won special favour, and so too has the product of the Arley Mine, which yields the well-known 'Wigan Wallsend', a bituminous coal, much esteemed as a gas coal and also for best household use. The Wigan coal is a steam coal of high repute, and is largely used in the ocean steamship trades.

Another of Thomas Taylor's underground photographs, taken in an unidentified Wigan colliery in 1898, and used by James Starr as the basis for a tinted postcard c.1905. The date of 15/12/98 can be seen on the roof beam.

The company operated not only the mines – and the iron works which burned a proportion of its coal – but also

Coal Mine – Miners working at Coal Seam

railway rolling stock, horse-drawn canal boats, and even steamers to move their annual output of six million tons around the country.

Electric lighting had been installed in many collieries before the end of the nineteenth century, but it was still sufficiently novel to be worth reporting. A 1901 account of the extensive coal workings around Aspatria, near Maryport, in present-day Cumbria noted that

In the early 1900s, Foxes Bridge Colliery, Cinderford, in the Forest of Dean, employed 641 people, 555 of them below ground. Foxes Bridge produced domestic coal, from seams which were repeatedly prone to flooding, and the mine came close to closing several times before production eventually ceased in 1931.

Coal has also been found, and is worked by the Brayton Demesne Colliery Co., whose pit commenced operations in 1869, drawing north and south, and working east and west. Brayton No. 4 pit was started in 1890. The output is 450 tons per day; the depth of shaft 560ft. In 1898 this pit was lit by electricity.

By the end of the Edwardian era, the colliery was operating five pits, and local photographer John Pattinson had produced a series of twenty-four postcards covering every aspect of the company's operations, amongst them a rare view of a group of Westmorland pit girls.

There was obviously a well-known and clearly-understood lexicon of coal types, with even relatively small local coal merchants enumerating the different coals they offered for sale, understanding that the names, types and characteristics of all of them were well known to their customers.

A contemporary advertisement for Seddon & Staveley, coal merchants in Bolton and agents for Messrs J. Blundell & Sons, another of the biggest mine owners in the area, promised their customers that

The quality of the coal supplied by this firm is of a very superior order, and comprises—Orrell, 4 feet, ditto 5 feet; ditto cobbles; ditto nuts. Pemberton 4 feet; ditto 5 feet; Wigan 4 feet; ditto 9 feet; King coal, ditto nuts. Gas, cannell. Hard coke; nut ditto. Orrell slack; Pemberton ditto; Wigan ditto; King ditto.

By 1907 when Lancashire output peaked, the county's

collieries were annually producing over 26 million tons from more than three hundred and fifty collieries – almost 10% of the national total, and nearly four times Britain's total output today. The Wigan coalfield alone accounted for around half that total. Just why the Wigan enjoyed a disproportionately high visibility in the postcard industry cannot be explained, but maybe it was just that photographers were attracted by the number of mines in a relatively small area, and the unusual make-up of the workforce.

At the same time, miners in the much larger South Wales coalfield annually brought to the surface more than 20% of the national output – but they featured on many fewer cards.

The Edwardian era was, however, fraught with difficulties for miners and their families – pressure from colliery owners to reduce wages led to an understandable increase in union membership, and increasing unrest amongst the colliers as income dropped and the cost of living rose.

Not surprisingly, local postcard publishers did their bit to ensure that the demonstrations, lockouts, strikes and riots which were triggered by that unrest all became the subjects of postcards which have become, today, important social history documents.

Although there had been many local strikes in the Edwardian years, the period is generally held to have been relatively free of industrial action, but as the decade drew to a close, tensions rose relentlessly.

Amidst the turmoil and unrest of the miners strike in Pontypridd, the contingent of the Metropolitan Police brought in to back up the local force still found time for a Christmas party which was, of course, recorded and published as a postcard.

THE CONQUERS OF ABERAMAN RIOTERS · ON THE·NIGHT OF NOV·21ST 1910

The grammar and spelling on locally produced cards sometimes fell short of what might be expected from the major national publishers, but they tell a vital part of the miners' stories.

What might, individually, have seemed like ripples on the waters of industrial peace, collectively amounted to a potentially much more fragile and dangerous situation. Unrest started to grow across Durham, Yorkshire, Lancashire, and the South Wales coalfield, and by the summer of 1910, it was reaching boiling point.

A considerable amount of unrest had arisen out of the implementation of a piece of legislation which had restricted the hours a miner was permitted to work.

Doncaster miners and their families taking part in a demonstration in June 1910.

MINERS' DEMONSTRATION DONCASTER JUNE 1910. 38

DUNRAVEN ST. TONYPANDY. AFTER THE STRIKE RIOT. 1910.

With considerable local interest generated by the strike, several photographers in Tonypandy were quickly to see the commercial value in producing short-run 'real photograph' postcards showing local scenes in its aftermath.

In place of the 'normal' 10 or 12 hour days which were commonplace, the Coal Mines Regulation (8 hours) Act of 1908 had the effect of reducing the take home pay of men who worked difficult seams – as earnings were usually dependent upon the amount of coal mined.

In some mines, the under-manager was permitted to make up wages to a reasonable sum, but in others all the hardships of reduced working hours fell on the colliers themselves.

With earnings dependent upon tonnage mined, the claims made by the Naval Colliery Company that workers in their Ely Pit in Pennygraig were mining too slowly made little sense, but the company locked out their entire workforce of 650 on 1 September 1910 – even those working other mines in the group – and brought in strike-breakers. Eventually police and soldiers were sent in to try and restore order, but their response served merely to spread unrest further. In Aberaman unrest escalated on the night of Thursday 21 November as the *Aberdare Leader* reported

> *Serious riots occurred on Tuesday evening; the strikers concentrated their attentions on the coal washeries, which were owned by the Powell Duffryn Colliery Co. It had not been anticipated that anything untoward in the district would happen in view of that fact that the dispute will shortly occupy*

*the attention of Coal Conciliation Board, and consequently the
dispute came as a surprise and very quickly the news spread
throughout the district that an attack was being made on the
washery.*

The arrival of the 18th Lancers on 9 November raised the
temperature further, until things reached a head twelve days
later.

*Some 200 or 300 people assembled outside the Aberaman
Institute and marched in a body to the storm centre, which is
situated between Cwmbach and Aberaman some mile and a
half from Aberdare. Many hundreds of women accompanied
the strikers. When within a few hundred yards of the washery
some 200 lads were dispatched as a sort of advance guard to
the washery, but they were turned to rout by the police. There
were about 30 policemen guarding the washery, but they did
not anticipate any serious trouble, and at the time when the
200 youths came on the scene a portion of the police were at
tea. They were, however, immediately summoned, and were
soon confronted by 2000 strikers, many of whom were armed
with sticks and other weapons.*

*The policemen ranged themselves in front of the power
house and the other premises but very quickly they were made
the object of a most hostile demonstration, and stones and*

A busy scene at
Aldwarke colliery
about two miles
north of Rotherham,
from a locally-
produced series of
postcards probably
dating from c.1908.
Aldewark Main
Colliery, the first
shaft for which had
been sunk in 1867,
was owned and
operated by John
Brown & Company,
the Sheffield steel-
makers who would
later achieve world-
wide fame as the
most famous
shipbuilders on
the Clyde.

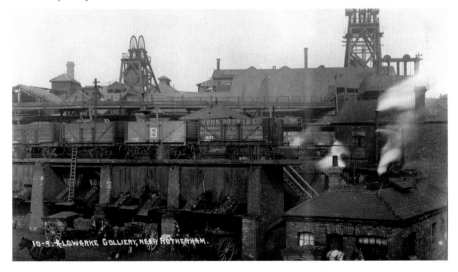

Below: As a result of the opening of Lower Duffryn Colliery, also known as the Cwmpennar Pit, in the first half of the nneteenth century, the rural landscape around Mountain Ash was changed irrevocably. Between 1841 and 1871, the population of the area – with the influx of miners and their families – increased more than tenfold to over 11,000 people. The pit closed in 1927.

Cwmpennar Colliery, Mountain Ash.

other missiles were hurled at them in a reckless manner and with a total disregard to life and limb or property.

The presence of the troops, arguably, both extended the strike and tilted the balance against any likelihood that the miners might win – something for which Winston Churchill as Home Secretary was widely held responsible, although he made no comment at the time. It took him until 1950 to address his role in the matter when he told a political meeting in Cardiff that

When I was Home Secretary in 1910, I had a great horror and fear of having to become responsible for the military firing on a crowd of rioters and strikers. Also, I was always in sympathy with the miners.

Churchill knew very well of course, as did every politician in those uncertain times towards the end of the Edwardian era, just how essential coal was in the maintenance of Britain's sea power, and that a prolonged period of unrest in the coal industry could have a devastating effect on the country's trade and influence. Britain was re-arming heavily, commissioning new faster and more powerful warships, increasing military demand for coal considerably. The merchant fleet on which the country depended so much

Opposite, top: A Thornycroft coal-fired steam lorry c.1902-04 being used for coal deliveries. Detail from a locally produced postcard published pre-1910.

Below: Miners at Brodsworth Colliery near Doncaster, c.1910. Judging by their clothes, they are not planning to start work anytime soon. The colliery had been opened in 1905, and two new shafts sunk in 1906 and 1907. It was one of the highest-producing mines in Yorkshire.

MICKLEY COAL CO (DRONFIELD) LTD NR TOTLEY ORPHANAGE DRONFIELD

to maintain its status as a world trading power was also growing rapidly.

Sympathy with the miners cause would, at the time, have been of secondary importance to keeping the rising cost of

MICKLEY COAL CO (DRONFIELD) LTD NR TOTLEY ORPHANAGE DRONFIELD

Left: Postcards were an ideal medium for advertising coal. This one, for William Perch & Co. was posted in 1908.

Below left: Mining Schools started to appear in the 1850s, and one of the first, the splendidly named Wigan & District Mining & Technical College, opened its doors in 1858 in a corrugated metal building to the right of the 'new' building seen here in 1903. The original school was built over its own mine-shaft. This fine 1902 building became Wigan Town Hall in the 1980s.

Opposite page: Two animated views in the pityard at the Mickley Coal Company, Dronfield as coal is loaded on to railway wagons, and down chutes on to horse-drawn wagons.

Overleaf: Titled 'Men ascending a Pit in Wales' this busy scene was photographed during one of the periods of industrial unrest around 1910 – under the watchful eye of a police sergeant.

coal to a minimum, and not something the very politically-aware Home Secretary would have voiced too loudly, if at all.

The political and social damage which had been done, however, would long endure, and bitterness in the mines would not go away.

The Tonypandy riots – also known as the Rhondda riots – prefaced a period of growing conflict within the coal industry which culminated eventually in the National Coal Strike of 1912, and demands for a national guaranteed wage.

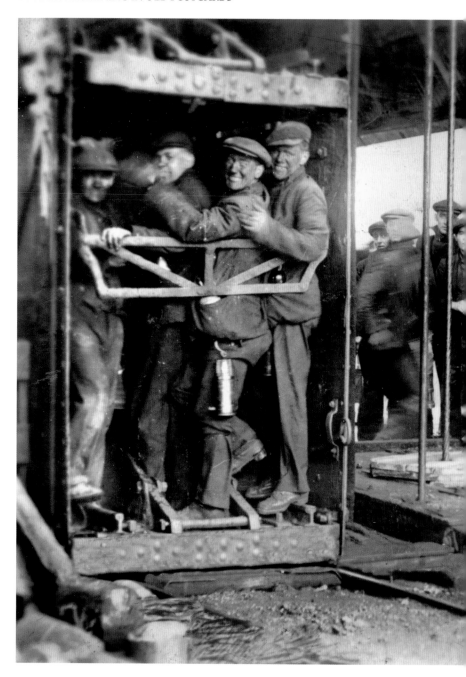

19. - LENS. - La descente au fond d'une mine

GOING UNDERGROUND

IN THE EARLIEST days of coal mining, the coal was recovered from seams close to the surface, but as demand for the fuel grew, and the potential profits to be made from its extraction increased, men were sent further and further underground in search of the best quality coal.

As early as the eighteenth century, deep mines had been dug at Culross in Fife by Sir George Bruce, their roadways extending well out under the River Forth. The depths of mine workings had increased exponentially during Victoria's reign, and by the time the Edwardian era dawned, shafts in excess of 2,000 feet were not uncommon. Considering the relatively primitive tools available to those who sunk them, such excavations represent significant feats of engineering, and prodigious physical effort on behalf of the navvies.

Some very detailed accounts survive of the sinking of mine shafts, and one in particular, from the New Venture Pit in Winstanley, Lancashire, in 1910 is particularly informative. It was written by Thomas Brooks, one of the 'winders' working on the sinking of the shaft.

Below: erecting pit props in an unidentified Wigan colliery, c.1904.

Opposite: Miners in an open bucket about to descend the mine shaft, Lens, France, 1906. It was common for stamps to be put on the front of early French postcards.

First the headgear and engine are fixed. Then they begin to dig a hole the size the shaft has to be until it is about 7 ft. deep. The sides are then lined with planks of wood, which are placed upright, and held in position by iron segments bolted securely together. This is called putting in the cribbing.

When rock is reached the compressed air drills are brought into operation and about 16 holes are drilled in one half of the pit bottom. These are then charged with explosives, time fuses are attached, which are coupled to an electric cable lowered from the surface. All the sinkers now ascend to the top.

The chargeman connects an electric battery to the cable, then he calls out 'fire', turns the battery handle and the shots go off like clockwork. Sometimes there is one misfires and this means no one shall descend the pit for one hour. After the shot-firing the safety lamp is lowered to the bottom to test for gas. The rock which is blasted up is now filled into the hoppets and sent to the surface whilst another 16 holes are being drilled in the other half of the pit bottom.

When the shaft is about 24 yards deep, preparations are made for lining the shaft with brickwork. The bricks used are blocks about 11 ins. long and 5 ins. thick slightly curved.

Opposite page: 'Waiting to go down the mine' – men working in a Barnsley colliery wait at the entrance to the cage to descend to the face at the start of their shift. *Regent Real Photo Series,* Barnsley c.1908.

Below: The lamp room at Atherton Colliery, Lancashire, on the edge of the Wigan Coalfield, photographed c.1907.

Miners working at the seam of a coal mine in Shamokin, Pennsylvania, a far cry from the cramped conditions at the face in British mines.

Holes are now drilled in the pit sides near the bottom, at equal distances and bars of 2 ins. round iron are driven into them, and are left projecting about 10 ins.

On these projecting portions, cast iron segments are fixed and securely bolted together. These are called "bricking rings" and are put in every 24 yards until the required depth of the shaft is reached. A strong wooden scaffold is now lowered to the pit bottom and is fixed on the cast iron segments and is held in position by strong moveable iron bars. A hoppet of mortar is now sent down which is turned over on the scaffold. This is done by the winding engine man in the following manner. The men in charge at the bottom unhook the chains from the top of the hoppet and hook them to rings near the bottom of the hoppet. Then they signal to the winder to stretch up and the hoppet is turned bottom upwards. They signal to lower down and the hoppet is turned right way up whilst being lowered.

This is also done with a hoppet of bricks. The winder is now kept very busy, raising lowering and winding up and down. When about 4 ft. of brickwork is put in all around the shaft, the scaffold is raised up and fixed on top of the brickwork and a further 4 ft. of brickwork is put in all artound the shaft. Tis goes on until all the brickwork is put into the top and when finished, sinking is then restarted, and all this goes on until the shaft is down to the required depth, 24 yards sinking and 24 yards bricking up.

The New Venture Pit shaft, 14 feet in diameter, eventually reached a depth of more than 1500 feet, and the bricks used to line the shaft were manufactured by Ormerod & Company at the nearby Orrell Brickworks.

The preferred explosive used in many Edwardian mine was a German invention known as 'Roburite', and in the case of the Lancashire coalfield, much of it was manufactured at the Roburite Explosive Company's works at Gathurst near Wigan.

Roburite was claimed to be much safer than the gunpowder or dynamite which had been widely used in the nineteenth century, and an 1892 advertisement for it detailed its properties – focusing on its value in the dusty and gaseous atmosphere of mines.

It was, according to the company, already used in England, Germany, Spain, Turkey and Australia. Indeed, it had first been trialled in Yorkshire in 1887, as reported in *The Scientific American* on 19 November.

A series of experiments of great interest and vital importance to colliery owners and all those engaged in mining coal has been carried out during the last ten days in the South Yorkshire coal field. The new mines regulation Act provides that any explosible used in coal mines shall either be fired in a water cartridge or be of such a nature that it cannot inflame firedamp. This indeed is

Sinking the shaft at the Victoria Pit, Standish, Lancashire. Work started early in 1900, and the shaft depth eventually reached 2000 feet. The colliery closed in 1959. By Thomas Brooks's account, this is clearly in the early stages of the development of the new shaft.

AU PAYS NOIR

N° 11. - La grande Veine

Toudi rimpli d'poussière,
Noir sus vinte, comme sus dos,
L'un saque el'carbon, l'tierre,
L'autre querch et ahu !!! pou l'tro
Poesie du Poète Mineur, A. LUCAS, de Lens

G. Moraux-Delannoy, phot.-editeur, Lens — Déposé

the problem which has puzzled many able chemists during the last few years, and which Dr. Roth, of Berlin, claims to have solved with his explosive "roburite." We recently gave a detailed account of trials carried out at the School of Military Engineering, Chatham, to test the safety and strength of roburite, as compared with gun cotton, dynamite, and blasting gelatine. The results were conclusive of the great power of the new explosive, and so far fully confirmed the reports of the able mining engineer and the chemical experts who had been sent to Germany to make full inquiries. These gentlemen had ample opportunity of seeing roburite used in the coal mines of Westphalia, and it was mainly upon their testimony that the patents for the British empire were acquired by the Roburite Explosive Company.

Miners going down the Shaft of Coal Mine.

from Harry B

Above: Miners going down the shaft of the Coal Mine – an undivided back postcard by the Universal Postal Card Company, New York & Leipzig, mailed in 1904.

Opposite: 'La Grande Veine' – a French card from c.1905, published in Lens, with a verse by 'A. Lucas de Lens', described on the card as a 'Poete Mineur'.

It has, however, been deemed advisable to give practical proof to those who would have to use it, that roburite possesses all the high qualities claimed for it, and hence separate and independent trials have been arranged in such representative collieries as the Wharncliffe Silkstone, near Sheffield, Monk Bretton, near Barnsley, and, further north, in the Durham coal field, at Lord Londonderry's Seaham and Silksworth collieries. Mr. G.B. Walker, resident manager of the Wharncliffe Colliery Company, had gone to Germany as an independent observer – provided with a letter of introduction from the Under Secretary of State for Foreign Affairs – and had seen the director of the government mines at Saarbruck, who gave it as his opinion that, so far as his experience had gone, the new explosive was a most valuable invention. Mr. Walker was so impressed with the great advantages of roburite that he desired to introduce it into his own colliery, where he gladly arranged with the company to make the first coal mining experiments in this country. These were recently carried out in the Parkgate seam of the Wharncliffe Silkstone colliery, under the personal superintendence of the inventor, Dr. Roth, and in the presence of a number of colliery managers and other practical men.

'Tunnel Entrance at Coal Mine'.

It is perhaps ironic that the Wharncliffe Silkstone Colliery would, in May 1914, be the scene of a second serious explosion in less than thirty years which cost eleven miners their lives. Indeed, it was as a direct result of an explosion in 1886 in which 22 miners had died, that the colliery manager William E. Garforth became interested in resolving the dangers which were associated with firing explosive charges in an environment heavy with coal dust. As will be seen later in this book, he became a pioneer in mine safety and rescue, and would also invent the WEG breathing apparatus which was used after several Edwardian colliery disasters.

'Tunnel Entrance at Coal Mine'. This card was in production from c.1904 until after 1914. Pennsylvanian coal companies operated many drift mines at that time.

It would appear that Roburite was first used in Lancashire in 1898 when the Prince Pit shaft for Blundell's Pemberton Collieries was being dug, a shaft which, with a diameter of 18 feet, eventually reached a depth of about 1300 feet. It was later narrowed to 15 feet diameter and continued downwards eventually reaching a depth of nearly 1800 feet.

The company's advertisements listed all the explosive's many useful properties for the mining industry.

Roburite is especially valuable on account of the perfect safety with which it may be handled, transported, and stored. Neither friction, percussion, nor heat will cause it to explode, and it is only when primed by a specially strong detonator that it can be exploded. It has the following special properties and advantages over all other explosives.

Roburite cannot be made to explode by concussion, by pressure, friction, nor by fire, lightning or electricity.

Roburite can be made to explode only by the insertion of a strong detonating cap into the cartridge, and is therefore perfectly safe and free from danger under all conditions of transit, storage, and handling.

Roburite contains no nitro-glycerine, and is therefore not subject to the excessive danger from change of temperature and thawing.

Roburite does not freeze.

Roburite may be hammered between two steel plates, and a red hot iron may be inserted into it, free from danger.
Roburite has the further advantage of giving off no noxious fumes, and not pulverising the material blasted, and miners may re-enter the galleries immediately after a shot is fired.
Roburite is practically flameless, and can be safely used in fiery mines, neither fine dust nor gases being exploded by it.

'Miners in the cage, going on shift', believed to have been photographed at Brodsworth Colliery, Yorkshire, and published as a postcard c.1910. Publisher unknown.

As will be seen later in this book, despite the efforts to improve the safety in British mines – including the use of an explosive which was claimed could not ignite gas or dust – there would continue to be explosions during shot-firing, at the cost of many miners' lives.

Despite the labour-intensive nature of the work, many pit shafts were sunk at a remarkable speed. In the Edwardian years, 50 feet a month was not uncommon, although that did mean a three-year project to sink a 1500 foot shaft – and a huge investment in manpower and materials before the first ton of coal could ever be extracted. By comparison, when Kellingley Colliery in North Yorkshire was sunk in the early 1960s, the shaft was dug and lined at a rate of well over 300 feet a month.

Right: Miners about to descend a mine in Pennsylvania c.1908.

Below: 'Bringing Coal to the Shaft', photographed c.1910 and published by Aspatria chemist John Pattinson. It offers a splendid view, illuminated by electric light deep underground. The exposure time must have been remarkably short, because unless they were fitted with blinkers pit ponies, used to living and working in the near darkness of the pit bottom, were often somewhat distressed by sudden bright light. This pony, however, has apparently been photographed too quickly to register any movement.

Although many of the Edwardian postcards of miners at work show them with picks and shovels working in cramped confined spaces, coal-cutting machinery was already being introduced into British collieries, hugely increasing the rate of extraction. Perhaps the image of the lone miner hacking away had more appeal to British postcard buyers.

In America, at the same time, postcards of underground workings were more likely to celebrate the latest technological advances, with heavy mechanical mining equipment to the fore, but such cards are rare in Britain before the Great War.

BRINGING COAL TO THE SHAFT   NO. 4 PIT, BRAYTON COLLIERIES

The North of England Institute of Mining & Mining Engineers visited the Margaret Pit of Newbottle Collieries near Houghton-le-Spring on 3 September 1902, and their visit was reported in the Institute's Journal. There they saw the very latest in coal-cutting equipment in action.

The Margaret pit is one of a group of nine pits comprising the Newbottle collieries, belonging to the Lambton Collieries, Limited. It is situated in the parish of Newbottle, about 1½ miles south-east of Penshaw station.

There are two pits, both of which are downcasts, one being 12 feet and the other 8 feet in diameter. This latter pit was sunk in 1774, and has been drawing coals continuously since that date.

The system of working in the Brass Thill seam is longwall, and in the other seams, bord-and-wall. The output is 800 tons per day.

There are 7 Lancashire boilers at this pit, each 8 feet in diameter, 30 feet long, and working at a pressure of 50 pounds per square inch. The boilers are fitted with Proctor mechanical stokers.

Electrically-driven coal-cutters – The generating-plant, which was not specially erected for driving the coal-cutting machines, has been in existence for several years for hauling, pumping and winding. It was installed in 1891, and except

COAL MINING. COLLIERS AT WORK.

No. 306 in 'Timothy's Series' of postcards by local Pentre photographer S. Timothy, c.1908, a group of miners photographed underground at Pentre Colliery, Glamorgan.

Left: A group of mine inspectors prepare to descend an American anthracite mine in 1908. Behind them stands one of the colliery locomotives.

Opposite page: A group of miners in a gateless cage preparing to go underground at Blue Fly Colliery, Riddings Lane, Wednesbury around 1890, photographed by Dr Edward Dingley, a local GP and keen amateur photographer. It was published as a tinted postcard c.1906 as was his study of pit wenches (p85). The card was published by Ryder & Son, printers and publishers, who also printed the local newspaper, the *Wednesbury Herald.*

for the renewals of certain parts, it remains exactly to-day as it was at that time.

The engines for driving the generating dynamos are of the Willans high-speed type, two in number, each being equal to 140 indicated horsepower, at a speed of 380 revolutions per minute. The steam-pressure is 80 pounds per square inch. Each engine has two cylinders, 17 inches in diameter, with a stroke of 8 inches. There are two generating dynamos, driven by means of link-leather belts, 18 inches wide, and each capable of giving out 80 amperes at a pressure of 780 volts, when running at a speed of 500 revolutions per minute: this is equal to an output of 84 horsepower.

The coal-cutters are of the diamond type of disc coal-cutter. Each cutter is driven by two series-wound motors at a pressure of 500 volts. The revolutions of the cutter-wheel are about 12 per minute. The diameter of the cutter-wheel, with cutters and boxes fixed, is 6 feet 4 inches. The average depth of the cut is usually a little over 5 feet, and the height of the cut is 48 inches. The power required to work each coal-cutter is on an average about 15 horsepower. Each machine is controlled by a reversing-switch fitted with resistances. The machine is drawn along the face, and kept up to its work by a rope-hauling arrangement, fixed to the end of the machine and worked by ratchet-gear from the driving-shaft.

Longwall mining involved cutting the coal from a continuous face which might be more than 1,000 feet long –

a system really only practicable with machine-cutting – while 'bord-and-wall' or bord-and-pillar' techniques involve mining coal from small 60-80 ft. sections often known as 'rooms'.

The 'Diamond' machine referred to at Newbottle was yet another piece of mining equipment designed by William E. Garforth and reportedly could, depending on the size of the disc in use, make the deepest cut of any coal-cutting machine in its day – cutting to a depth of more than 5 feet.

Other types of machines, using percussion techniques and manufactured by Patterson and by Hardy & Siskol were also in widespread used by 1905, the type and size of machine being dependent upon the depth of the seam and the type of coal being mined. Disc-based machines were ideally suited to 'longwall' mining, while the pneumatic percussive machines found widespread use in mines using a 'room' based approach.

As mines went ever deeper, the conditions under which the miner laboured became more demanding. Quite apart from the physical distances they had to travel to reach their workplaces, there were other issues.

'Endless Haulage at No. 4 Pit Brayton Collieries', another card from the series of 24 photographed c.1910 and published by Aspatria chemist John Pattinson.

ENDLESS HAULAGE AT NO.4 PIT, BRAYTON COLLIERIES

Writing in his 1912 book *Coal; its origin, method of working, and preparation for market*, Francis H Wilson wrote

The Royal Commission on Coal Supplies, 1903-05, took 4,000 feet as the limit of depth. At the Pendleton Collieries in Lancashire the workings are now over 3,200 feet from the surface, and at the Produits Colliery in Belgium a depth of 3,773 feet has been reached. With the continued improvements in mining methods and machinery, there is every reason to believe that the 4,000 feet limit will not prove an unsurmountable obstacle. The pressure of the strata at this depth will certainly be enormous, but whilst this may decrease the percentage of round coal and increase the cost of maintaining the roadways and of timbering, it should assist in the working of the coal.

The great difficulty of deep working is the increase in temperature and the humidity of the air. There does not appear to be a uniform rate of increase of temperature with depth, though in this country the rate of increase is found to be approximately 1 degree Fahrenheit for every 60 feet of depth.

Tilmanstone Colliery in Kent was sunk into some very difficult and wet geology. Work started in 1906 and progressed slowly. In 1909 a hoist bucket fell down the shaft, killing three men and cutting through the pump pipes. Thousands of gallons of water a minute poured into the pit. Judging by the oilskins on the men in the hoppit, and the sombre onlookers, this card may date from that accident. Work on sinking the shaft started again in 1910 but the first coal was not brought to the surface until 1913.

TILMANSTONE COLLIERY

HEROES OF THE MINE. (4)

The gallant deeds of these Heroes,
The limit, there's no one can tell,
At Pretoria pit and Whitehaven too,
Many a brave collier fell;
And when the "Peacemaker"— King Edward,
Who, through God's mercy now lies at rest,
Awarded his MEDAL OF VALOUR,
'Twas to heroes the bravest and best.

WORDS BY PERMISSION OF THE LAWRENCE WRIGHT MUSIC Co.,
29, CONDUIT STREET, LEICESTER.

The fourth card in the series *Heroes of the Mine* – published just a few weeks after the death of King Edward VII – included in its verse a reference to the recently deceased king, and his Edward Medal, the Medal of Valour.

It is quite possible to work in dry air at a temperature of 95 Fahrenheit; in fact the temperature of the lower workings at the Pendleton Collieries is 93½ Fahrenheit, but in moist air the limit of working is reached at about 80 Fahrenheit, as at this temperature workmen are very soon fatigued.

The problem of temperature and humidity will no doubt be overcome to a great extent by the passing of large volumes of dry air through the workings of deep mines on even a more elaborate scale than is done at present, and it is quite possible that some means will be devised of cooling the air and reducing its temperature before it enters the workings.

But more powerful fans brought their own problems, especially in mines where spontaneous outbreaks of fire were commonplace.

This was a particular problem in several of the collieries in the Fife coalfield, and heroism in the face of just such an incident brought about the decoration of two local miners, George and James Dryburgh, when the King awarded them the newly instituted Edward Medal, an award which had been specifically commissioned to recognise bravery in Britain's mines and industrial complexes.

After a spontaneous fire in a disused part of the mine, the workings were filled with clouds of what the miners referred to as "coal stink" but was officially described as "an excess of Carbonic Acid gas, and when this excess had passed off, Carbon Monoxide came off in large volume". Their bravery was report in *The Times* on 22 July 1908,

As will be seen from the Court Circular, the King yesterday at Buckingham Palace decorated nine miners and a seaman with medals for bravery. The miners who received the Edward Medal for Bravery in Mines were John Henry Thorne, Joseph Outram, Waiter Clifford, James Cranswick, James Hopwood, James Whittingham, George Dryburgh, James Dryburgh, and Morgan Howells.

In respect of the two Dryburghs who although bearing the same name are not related, they are the first recipients from Scotland of Edward medals. They were engaged at the Wemyss Collieries, East Fife, on December 29 last, when a fire broke out. The two men descended the shaft to rescue their comrades, several of whom perished in the disaster. George Dryburgh was overcome by the fumes and James Dryburgh dragged him along the passage and held him in the cage until the surface was reached. Subsequently other men went down the shaft, and the jury at the inquest recommended eight miners' names for the medal. The Home Secretary, in conference with the Inspector of Mines in the district, finally selected the two Dryburghs for the honour.

Thorne, Outram, Clifford, Cranswick, Hopwood and Whittingham were part of the rescue team at Hamstead Colliery in Birmingham on 4 March 1908, and Howells was honoured as a result of his bravery at Seven Sisters Colliery, Neath.

Mining disasters were, sadly, commonplace in Edwardian Britain, and are featured in the final chapter of this book. As will be seen, postcards invariably featured those who had been killed in accidents below ground, so cards which featured 'heroes' whose bravery did not cost them their lives must have been a refreshing change.

The Edward Medal was a rarely-used honour, being awarded fewer than 600 times before finally being withdrawn from the list of honours in 1971.

Mechanisation of mining was seen as an essential part of both the need to increase output and the quest for improved safety – both goals dominated the Edwardian era as Britain rushed to meet the growing demand for fuel. Mining, however, always remained a highly dangerous way of earning a living.

Coal output did not reach its peak until 1913, by which time the nation's collieries had a workforce exceeding 1.1 million men and women.

Looking rather less than happy to be photographed and featured in a postcard, George and James Dryburgh, the heroes od the Wemyss fire rescue, pose outside Buckingham Palace after becoming two of the first recipients of the Edward Medal on 21 July 1908. They had gone down the fume-filled mine to try and rescue colleagues after a fire on 29 December 1907.

AMAZONS AT THE PIT BROW

WHILE MOST OF Britain's coalfields had an exclusively male workforce by 1900, several areas had a tradition of employing women on the pithead coal screens. When Queen Victoria came to the throne, women and children were widely used in all aspects of mining work, but their employment underground had been outlawed by 1842! Known as 'pit girls' or 'pit brow lasses', these women sorted and graded the coal, removing stone as the coal rattled past them down chutes, on conveyor belts or over grading screens. They were also used to push coal trucks around the pit yard, and load railway wagons and canal barges, their massive shovels giving a hint of the loads they could manhandle.

The coal screens at Pemberton Collieries, one of Wigan's largest mines. c.1905.

The pit brow lass has no counterpart today. She was one of the most visible of colliery workers and, by the heavy nature of the work she did, she was a constant source of curiosity and fascination. These women proved daily that no amount of hard physical work was too great for them.

Ever since the earliest days of photography, fascination with working women had brought these powerful 'pit brow lasses' in front of countless cameras.

Despite less than pleasant working conditions, and arduous physical labour, they earned poor wages. At between nine and twelve shillings a week – depending on the task they performed – in the years before the Great War, their pay did not compare well with their male counterparts who earned twenty-seven shillings a week, and even less favourably with the men working underground who, by comparison, could earn nearly two pounds a week. So perhaps it was to earn a little more money – as well as local fame – that the women posed proudly in their working clothes for the photographers employed by local postcard producers.

Many pit brow lasses came from families with long mining traditions, their grandmothers and great grandmothers having worked underground. Little more than sixty years before these postcards were published, tens of thousands of women and children had been employed below the surface in Britain's hundreds of mines.

The coal tubs provided an ideal platform for this group of Moss Hall workers posing for a postcard published by Will Smith of Wigan.

When the Victorian eccentric Arthur Munby first visited the Wigan coalfield in the 1860s, as part of his enduring fascination with working women, he could not believe the size of the women he encountered, pushing huge coal tubs and baskets around the pit yard. He was in awe of the size of the shovels they wielded, and the weights they could lift!

Himself a large man, Munby felt dwarfed by the women he met, and fascinated by their work. He was fascinated too by the transformation which they wrought when their work was over, changing from working giant during the day, to very feminine wife and mother at home during the evenings and at the weekend.

He commissioned many local photographers to take pictures of the women, collecting and filing them alongside pictures of their counterparts in the French and Belgian coalfields, fisher-women from Yorkshire and elsewhere, and servant girls from London.

Munby, however, was not unique in his fascination – Manchester-born Frances Hodgson Burnett's first successful book, *That Lass o' Lowrie's*, published in 1877, celebrated the life and dreams of the fictional character Jean Lowrie, a pit brow lass who had aspirations!

Notoriously difficult to read – the dialogue is written almost entirely in dialect and is only easily understandable if read aloud – *That Lass o' Lowrie's* never had the enduring success of her better-known works, *The Secret Garden* and *Little Lord Fauntleroy*. But Burnett was totally enthralled by the idea of women undertaking such work. In writing her book, she had to create spellings

Wigan pit girls had been posing for the camera since the cartes-de-visite of the 1860s. Robert Little took many photographs of the pit girls, and sold them widely – including several to Arthur Munby.

for a language which was always spoken but rarely written down!

Making it all the more surprising that she was writing in a northern dialect, Burnett had emigrated to America by that time, although she did return regularly to her native North of England.

In the first few paragraphs of the book, she presented an image of the pit girls which was not entirely complementary – an image which the story itself dispelled as the warmth of the characters was evolved and developed.

They did not look like women, or at least a stranger new to the district might easily have been misled by their appearance as they stood together in a group by the pit's mouth. There were about a dozen of them – all "pit girls," as they were called; women who wore a dress more than half masculine, and who talked loudly and laughed discordantly, and some of whom, God knows, had faces as hard and brutal as the hardest of their collier brothers and husbands and sweethearts. They had lived their lives among the coal-pits, and had worked early and late at the "mouth," ever since they had been old enough to take part in the heavy labour. It was not to be wondered at that they had lost all bloom of womanly modesty and gentleness. Their mothers had been "pit girls" in their time, their grandmothers in theirs; they had been born in coarse homes; they had fared hardly, and worked hard; they had breathed in the dust and grime of coal, and, somehow or other, it seemed to stick to them and reveal itself in their natures as it did in their bold, unwashed faces. At first one shrank from them, but one's shrinking could not fail to change to pity. There was not an element of softness to rule or even influence them in their half savage existence.

On the particular evening of which I speak, the group at the pit's mouth were even more than usually noisy. They were laughing, gossiping, and joking – coarse enough jokes – and now and then a listener might have heard an oath flung out

Ever since the first carte-de-visite photographs of pit brow women were put on sale in the 1860s, a recurrent theme was the size of the shovels which they used.

Overleaf: Pit brow lasses at work, Moss Pit, Ince, 1905. The men watching were the colliery weighmen.

81

Detail from a Belgian postcard, c.1910, showing a female pit worker in a huge colliery complex. As in parts of Britain, women continued to work in Belgian coal yards until well after the Second World War.

Below: An advertisement for Will Smith of Wigan showing the frontage of his newsagent's shop in Wigan Lane, c.1909. Smith styled himself as 'The Postcard King', and his series of Wigan postcards numbered more than 100, including many of the pit girls at work. The shop windows are festooned with his cards. The shop is still a newsagent's today.

carelessly, and as if all were well used to the sound. Most of them were young women, though there were a few older ones among them, and the principal figure in the group – the centre figure about whom the rest clustered – was a young woman. But she differed from the rest in two or three respects. The others seemed somewhat stunted in growth; she was tall enough to be imposing. She was as roughly clad as the poorest of them, but she wore her uncouth garb differently. The man's jacket of fustian, open at the neck, bared a handsome, sun-browned throat. The man's hat shaded a face with dark eyes that had a sort of animal beauty, and a well-moulded chin. It was at this girl that all the rough jokes seemed to be directed.

Over a century later another American, Martin Cruz Smith, best known for *Gorky Park*, developed similar themes when he wrote his 1996 novel *Rose* – the story of Rose Molineux, a pit brow lass, and her highly improbable friendship with the daughter of the mine-owner.

By the early 1900s, the role of the woman worker in the coal industry was restricted to the washeries, the screens and the coal tubs at the pithead – physically demanding, and only manageable by such powerfully built women.

Despite the fact that the vast majority of postcards showing 'pit brow lasses' were taken in and around Wigan, women did similar work across the British coalfields. Only a very few cards have been identified from South Wales, Westmorland or the Midlands, with none, so far, from the coalfields of Yorkshire, Kent, Shropshire, the North-East or Scotland.

Certainly there were plenty of women employed in other coalfields, so were Wigan publishers simply more entrepreneurial than others?

On the coal screens, the role of women was to break up the larger lumps and remove the stone which often accompanied it as the coal moved past them on the screens.

In the coalfields of the Black Country the women were known as 'Pit Bank Wenches'. Their work was the same, although very many fewer postcards celebrated their lives. This photograph, taken at Blue Fly Colliery, Riddings Lane, Wednesbury in 1890 was the work of local GP Dr Edward Dingley. It was published as a plain postcard in 1904, and as a tinted one in 1906.

One of the best known tinted postcards of Wigan pit brow lasses, this view was photographed at the Junction Colliery, Abram, and was available in sepia or tinted as here. Published by Will Smith, it was printed in Germany.

Trieuses de Charbon –
coal sorters or
graders – from a
photograph taken at
Montceau-les-Mines
in the Bourgogne
region of Eastern
France, and
published locally
by Maison de
Magazins Réunis.
In Edwardian times
over two million
tons a year was
extracted from the
Montceau coalfield.

Opposite: Published
by James Starr, this
postcard shows one
of the women who
worked for Haigh
Collieries, wearing
the distinctive
uniform of tartan
shawl and wide
bonnet. Tradition
has it that the
uniform was
designed by the
wife of the owner,
the Earl of Crawford
and Balcarres.

MONTCEAU-les-MINES. - Trieuses de Charbon

des Magasins Réunis

Elsewhere in the yard they emptied the tubs which came up from the face, loaded the railway wagons, or tipped the loaded tubs into the barges which waited alongside adjacent canal wharfs.

The widespread fascination which the pit brow girls held for people from all walks of life had a curious impact upon them. As figures of some curiosity, and often the subjects of photography, a few deliberate fashion considerations crept into their daily dress.

Sylvia Pankhurst, daughter of Emmeline, wrote extensively about the women in the journal *Votes for Women* in August 1911 – recalling her visit to the Wigan coalfield in 1907

The term Pit Brow Lassies includes the Bankswomen, the Pit Brow Lassies proper, and the Sorters or Screen Women. In some collieries all threes three classes of women are employed; in others only the Pit Brow Lassies and the Sorters; and in others again only the Sorters. Let us deal first with the work of the bankswomen. They stand, two of them, at the mouth of the shaft that reaches down into the mines below. As the cage laden with coal-filled tubs (tubs are square boxes on wheels) comes to the surface and then stops, they enter it, and between them drag the tubs out one by one, and with a hard push send them rolling off along some railway lines. This work is sometimes done by men, sometimes by women, and one may sometimes see a banksman and bankswoman standing together at the shaft working the same number of hours, and performing their equal share of the same task, but while a banksman is paid from 4s.9d. to 5s. a day a bankswoman gets only from 1s.10d. to 2s.4d.

The tubs roll off at the push of a banksman or bankswoman, and are met as they come by a group of pit brow lassies, who push and drag and guide them on their way to the sorting

screens. The wages for pit brow lassies range from 1s.6d. to 2s. or 2s.6d. a day. In some cases, one woman with a knowledge of coal is stationed at a point to which all the tubs must come and wait at which the lines leading to the various screens diverge. Here, according to the size and quality of the coal which it contains, she decides in which direction each tub must go, turning the points for it, and pushing it on towards the received into which it is emptied, and from whence the coal falls to the sorting screen.

'Colliery Girl 15', a pit brow lass from an unidentified colliery, c.1905, photographer and publisher unknown.

The sorting screens are in the form of long belts, which move continually and carry the coal along with them. They are usually some 3 feet wide, and about 3 feet from the ground. On either side of the belts rows of women stand picking out pieces of stone, wood, and other waste stuff from amongst the coal as it slowly moves past. Sometimes they pick out the waste pieces with their fingers, sometimes they catch at them with an iron hook or rake, and sometimes with a hammer they strike off those which may be adhering to the coal itself. Some collieries supply many more tools for coal sorting than others do, where most of the work is done with the fingers. Serious accidents on the pit brow are now rare, but minor accidents on fingers, caused frequently by the slipping of large piece of coal upon them, are now more common. The dust from the coal is constantly rising, and the women's faces, hands and clothing

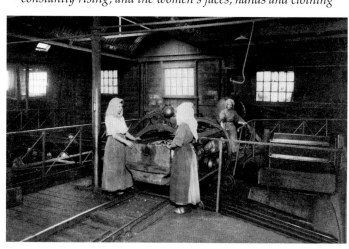

A postcard published c.1910 by Thill of Brussells and titled *Le Charbonnage – Déversement d'un chariot de charbon sur les appareills de criblage à l'aide d'un embuteur actionée mécaniquement.*

Showing unusual familiarity for the time, women workers pose with their male colleagues at the pithead at Pochin Colliery, Tredegar, South Wales, c.1906.

are soon blackened by it. Their heads are closely muffled in shawls to protect their hair. In some cases the belt is so arranged that it is necessary for two women to kneel on the ground at each end of it to attend to the aperture by which the coal passes off the belt, and to prevent it becoming clogged. The women who sort the coal are usually paid 1s.6d. a day, though girls and those who are learning get less, and some get as much as 2s. a day.

The sorting of coal entails practically no physical exertion, but the work of the bankswomen, and pit brow lassies neces-sitates great muscular strength and power of endurance. Both of these things they possess in abundant measure. Indeed,

Overleaf: A Louis Levy card from c.1905 from the series 'Mines et Mineurs', and titled *Au Triage* shows the French screen girls – Trieuses – posing in the midst of their coal screens, together with a male supervisor and, perhaps, a manager. The card was posted from Montceau-les-Mines in 1907.

Pit props and pit brow lasses in the yard at Strangeways Hall, Hindley, c.1905, photographed by Thomas Taylor, and published by James Starr.

Below: On the screens at an unidentified Lancashire colliery c.1908.

Bottom: Women moving coal tubs in the yard at the Moss Hall Colliery Company's Arley Pit in Ince. The double tub hoists can be seen to the right. Here the tubs are being moved on metal sheets, not rails.

when one sees them working side by side with men, they appear almost stronger than the men. They are many of them splendidly made, lithe and graceful, and, including the sorters, for all the coal dust, have clear, fresh complexions. Their rosy cheeks contrast strangely with the wan white faces of their sisters in the neighbouring cotton mills.

The women themselves were aware of the health hazards of the damp interiors of cotton mills. 'My father was pleased when I came to work on the pit brow' one coal sorter told Miss Pankhurst, 'because it brought me out so.'

When she asked what 'brought out' meant, the girl replied that since going to work at the pit she had felt and looked stronger and brighter than before. Local doctors, apparently, regularly recommended 'getting t'pit' as a cure for the ill-health endured by so many girls in the weaving sheds!

Initially attired in heavyweight fabrics, and sackcloth aprons – the sort of robust clothing necessary to withstand the rigour of their work – the girls were often the subject of criticism due to their lack of femininity. Indeed, it was suggested that there was a moral consequence of expecting men to work alongside women dressed in trousers – for many of the Wigan pit girls traditionally wore breeches

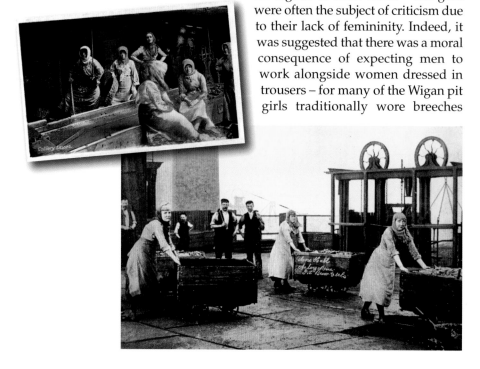

92

In working costume.   In ordinary costume.

Wigan pit brow lasses.

Five pit brow lassies pose for the camera in their working attire, left, (and in a tinted card below) while, right, their appearance in their 'Sunday Best' celebrates their femininity. Postcards which compared 'work' and 'leisure' views of working women were very popular in Edwardian times.

and short skirts rather than long skirts and leggings. Questions in Parliament in the 1860s had suggested that the effect on men of such working arrangements might actually be unhealthy – and as well as the effect on the morals of the male workforce in having women working alongside them in male attire, there was the corruption of the women themselves appearing in public thus dressed!

Really, these were just side issues, and the key question was about whether or not women should be employed in such rough work at all – the male clothes issue was just an opportunity for the newspapers of the day to create a good story.

The wearing of 'breeches' was largely a Wigan custom – although widely accepted across many parts of Europe. In collieries in the Midlands, Yorkshire, the Midlands and South Wales, the women usually wore calf-length heavy dresses, while many of their counterparts in the Belgian coalfield had been wearing trousers since before the middle of the nineteenth century – although those seen in early twentieth century postcards are invariable wearing dresses.

PIT BROW GIRLS

But in Belgium and parts of France, women continued to be able to work underground for half a century after they had been banned from British mines.

Indeed, one of the central characters in Emile Zola's 1885 novel *Germinal*, Catherine Maheu, worked underground pushing coal tubs from the coalface to the bottom of the shaft and back.

Getting ready for her shift at the mine, Zola wrote that Catherine.

stepped into her miner's trousers, put on her coarse linen jacket and fastened her blue cap over the knot in her hair. In these clean, Monday-morning clothes, she looked like a little man, and the only trace of her sex was a slight swing of the hips.

A studio portrait of a pit brow lass, by Thomas Taylor of Platt Bridge, c.1905, and published as a postcard by Will Smith.

In England, such attire would surely have been considered an affront to Christian decency – but of course by that time the idea of women working in the near-total darkness of the pit bottom was considered barbaric!

In the south Lancashire coalfields around Haydock, the women worked on the pit brow with long dresses and multiple petticoats! Between the two customs, the Black Brook was a dividing line – with the girls in 'kirtles' to the south openly admitting that they would be mortally ashamed to be seen dressed in breeches in the manner adopted by their northern counterparts!

There were several attempts to completely outlaw the employment of women on the brow, most notably in 1887 and again in 1911. Both attempts were defeated, and on both occasions Lancashire women travelled to London to participate in the protests against the planned legislation.

In 1885, the pit brow women found a strong ally in the local HM Inspector of Mines who wrote in his annual report that,

Their moral character has been so gratuitously libelled and their working dress pronounced bold and unbecoming. So far as my observation has gone, I have seen no good reasons for legislation to prevent these women earning a livelihood at the occupation they have chosen; they always appear orderly and industrious, and it is a favourite employment.

A Veteran Coal Sorter.

The Wrench Series. No. 3733

By the time the postcard era came along in the early 1900s, fashion differences between coalfields were less marked, with the long rough skirt worn over leggings being the norm, and with relatively few collieries still dressing their pit lasses in breeches. Trousers and aprons remained the order of the day in several collieries around Wigan, but in few others. There was no drab uniformity in their working clothes, however – the wives of colliery owners delighted in creating local 'uniforms' which distinguished their pit girls from those of other companies. The Haigh Collieries, owned by the Earl of Crawford and Balcarres, dressed their girls in a plaid tweed shawl or scarf to reflect the owner's Scottish heritage.

E. Caustier, a contemporary French writer, noted in *Les Entrailles de las Terre* in 1902 that the style of dress was very similar to that in French mines.

Above: A 'Wrench Series' postcard from c.1905 using a late Victorian photograph of a surprisingly elderly pit brow worker. Most had left the screens by their thirties when they married and started families. Few returned later in life.

Left: Pit Brow Lasses at Brayton Domain Colliery, Aspatria. In Westmorland collieries, the coal screens were known as 'Picking Bands'.

No. 12.   **PICKING BANDS.**
Pit-brow lasses picking inferior coal and dirt from the coal as it travels into wagons ready for the market.
BRAYTON DOMAIN COLLIERIES   NO. 4 PIT. BRAYTON

The Screen Room at Chanters Colliery, Atherton, 1905. Mining in the area can be traced back to the seventeenth century, but today the site of Chanters Colliery is an industrial estate. The main shaft at the colliery had been deepened to 2000 feet just four years earlier, to reach the Arley Seam, one of the richest in the Lancashire coalfield.

Their costume, in other ways very simple, consists of a type of trouser which only just covers the knee, and which has a very short skirt over it which is almost hidden by an apron whose light colour, sometimes white, makes a singular contrast in all the sombreness; they wear over the top half a Scottish shawl of various colours and design. Finally, they wear on their heads a type of hat which protects them from the coal dust. It must be added that they wear on their feet a kind of boot, the upper part being in leather, but whose sole being extremely thick is often made of wood.

The Atherton pit brow lasses card, *above*, was used as an advertisement for a Manchester coal merchant in September 1906, when best quality coal cost less than a pound a ton – with bags costing extra.

In most mines, though, the standard headgear was a woven scarf or shawl, and the standard footwear was the clog. He also observed that the women were not all like the Amazons who would be depicted in the postcards just a few years later. "The frail limbs and childlike faces of some of them," he wrote, "indicate that only light work could humanely be asked of them, so that concentration plays a greater part in their work than muscular effort."

In the Victorian era, fascination with the working pit women had shown no signs of abating, despite many attempts to outlaw the work.

In an article in *The Penny Pictorial Magazine* in 1899, illustrated by Herbert Wragg – whose studio

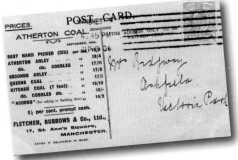

portrait photographs of the Wigan pit brow lasses would later reappear as a series of postcards – Arthur Birnage had prematurely predicted their imminent disappearance.

Had his prediction proved correct, the numerous and remarkable series of postcards of Edwardian pit girls from several publishers which appeared in the decade afterwards would never have been produced nor handed down to us.

In a few years time it is more than likely that there will not be a single girl collier in the country. Probably not one person in ten is aware that girl colliers exist today, so that when total prohibition of this kind of labour does come to pass the public mind will not be greatly disturbed. [His prediction was out by more than half a century!]

The reason for this lack of knowledge is easily explained. In the year 1840 there was a great agitation on this subject, which resulted in a law that made the labour of women in the coal mines illegal. Up to that period women were even allowed to go down the mines with their husbands and brothers; and in this connection it is interesting to note that even to-day, in

Above: This tinted Milton series postcard c.1906 from an earlier photograph, originally appeared as a sepia postcard by Wrench c.1904

Left: Women at work in the covered yard at Douglas Bank Colliery, c.1905. The metal sheets on the ground are believed to be there for use in spot inspections of the quality of the screened coal. The contents of a tub would be emptied on to the sheets for checking.

This tinted postcard view of Blundell's Pemberton Colliery, published 1905, is based on a late Victorian photograph by James Millard.

Belgium and some parts of Germany, female toil of this description is still allowed.

There were, he estimated "still some two or three thousand girl colliers" in British pit yards, mainly in Wigan and Shropshire, and that their ages ranged from 12 to 22. That the majority of them were in the South Lancashire coalfield was understood.

Birnage's account of the wage structure echoed that of Sylvia Pankhurst, and he too commented on the inherent inequality, and noted that "the men, who practically perform the same kind of work, get about double the wages."

Coal sorters on the screens at Strangeways Hall, Hindley photographed by Thomas Taylor, and published by James Starr.

Like the workers in the factories they have to commence their toil at six o'clock in the morning, and, with the exception of rests for breakfast and dinner, they keep at it until four o'clock in the afternoon. The hours are thus rather long, and it is a good thing that, as a class, the girls are hardy, for they have to work in all weathers. On a wet day they present a remarkable appearance, their faces begrimed with the coal dust.

But the most amusing side to the life of these female colliers is their pit dress. As will be seen by our illustrations, it is very difficult in some cases to believe that they are not men. Ordinarily the problem is quite as great, and if it were not for the tucked-up skirt and the voice – though it is not always possible to be guided by the latter – some of them would pass without much trouble as brawny, well-proportioned members of the sterner sex.

Colliery Girl.

Another of the studio portraits of Wigan Pit Brow Lasses published by James Starr. This was probably photographed in Millard's Studio in Market Street c.1904, continuing a traditional market for such portraits which local photographers had enjoyed since the late 1860s and the era of the carte-de-visite.

Over the head they wear a soft bonnet, which fits very tightly on their hair. In addition to their shawl, they are robed in cloth jacket, which, in the majority of cases, belonged to their father or brother, but now discarded by them as being too shabby. On the knees of the short trousers that they wear is a patch for kneeling purposes, and during their work the petticoats are tucked up in the manner shown in the illustrations. It is interesting to learn, however, that, although their attire and labour is of a manly character, there the resemblance ends, and all that is truest and best in womanhood may be seen in the lives of the majority of these young women who gain their livelihood at the pit brow.

Two years later, the unnamed contributor of a sometimes inaccurate article entitled *The Pit Broo Lassies of Lancashire* in the 30 November 1901 issue of the magazine *Black and White Budget* estimated the number of pit girls in South Lancashire alone at about a thousand higher than the national total estimated by Birnage. He also suggested a slightly different age range.

Two views of Colliery Girls at Work in on the Picking Belts at Standish Collieries, Lancashire, probably photographed by James Millard of Market Street in Wigan in the 1890s. In most pit girl cards, the girls are standing reasonably erect, but in the upper card they are bent double over the moving belts. It must have been back-breaking work. The tinted postcard was published as No. 44 in James Starr's Series, c.1904. The publisher of the upper view is unknown.

The costume of the pit-brow girl is unique. And, apart from that, the girls themselves are fascinating as a class performing a peculiar kind of work at the collieries in the South-West Lancashire coal district. Some 3,000 or 4,000 girls are employed at the various pits in that region, but, except for a few in Shropshire, there are none in other parts of the country. In age they range, as a rule, from fourteen to twenty-five years, and they are paid at the rate of less than two shillings a day on the average for work which men do for four shillings or more.

Now while the number of women employed in the pityards of Staffordshire, Westmorland, South Wales and elsewhere may not have rivalled the numbers in Lancashire, they must have totalled a considerable figure.

This writer also gives a different interpretation of the dress code adopted by the girls, suggesting that it had been dictated as much by practicality outside the pityard as it was inside.

It will be seen from the photographs that the girls work in trousers. At several pits the costume is so modified that wear aprons which cover the masculine garments referred to, but this is a recent idea, as up to a comparatively short time ago the women tucked up to the waist the skirt which they assume for the purpose of going to and from work.

Colliery Girls at Work.

Altogether, the dress is practical, and enables the girls to go about their work with the freedom of movement which is necessary and which could not otherwise be obtained.

The implication was clear – being seen in trousers outside the workplace was not something the women would ever countenance. Whatever their working appearance, away from the colliery, and after a good bath, they were unmistakedly feminine.

Men were not driven to acts of uncontrollable passion on seeing them dressed in trousers, as predicted by those who feared for the moral welfare of the girls.

Their young suitors even wrote poems about them, including what is probably the best known one today. Short and to the point, it said it all.

Her face besmeared with coal-dust, as black as black can be,
She is a pit brow lassie, but she's all the world to me.

Above: The uniform worn by the women at Lamb & Moore's Colliery, Wigan, photographed by Herbert Wragg c.1905.

Just how many women were needed in each pit yard to work the screens was dependent upon the amount of stone brought to the surface along with the coal, and yet despite

Left: At work on the picking belts in the screen room at Victoria Pit, Standish, c.1910. Sinking the Victoria's shaft had only been completed in 1903, so this scene is relatively early in the colliery's productive life. Here, as opposite, the girls are virtually bent double over the belts.

101

Pit women from an unidentified Lancashire colliery. from the 'Milton Series' of postcards of Colliery Lasses.

the often large numbers employed in this filthy work, washing and toilet facilities for them were poor.

Women's pithead baths were largely non-existent before the 1930s! But the same was the case for the majority of the men who worked underground in many pits into the 1920s.

By the outbreak of the Second World War, women were more usually employed solely in the coal washeries, and that remained their major working environment until they generally disappeared from the coalfields in the late 1950s. A few continued to work into the 1960s, and the last female surface worker in any British colliery had gone by 1970.

With their departure, a unique and fascinating chapter in the history of working women in Britain closed – but our fascination with the women and their work continues.

Pit lasses at Strangeways Hall Colliery, 1905. In the front sit young girls, probably straight out of school, starting their career on the coal screens.

Across the coalfields, since women finally left the pityard, the unique stories of the last of the pit brow girls have been recorded for posterity by local historians, but very few first-hand accounts survive of their Edwardian predecessors.

Their enduring celebrity was assured, but we will never know how many photographs were taken, or how many postcards of them were produced during the Edwardian years.

Today the industry which employed them has, itself, all but disappeared. Only these postcards and photographs survive to tell the stories of Britain's 'Amazons at the pit brow' as they had once been described in the Victorian magazine *The Leisure Hour*.

Five pit brow women photographed by Thomas Taylor, probably at Bamfurlong Colliery, later published as a postcard by Will Smith.

DON'T GO DOWN IN THE MINE, DAD

Above: 'I dreamt that I saw the pit all afire' – lantern slide 4 from Bamforth's 20-slide series to accompany the song *Don't Go Down The Mine, Dad.*

IN EDWARDIAN times the dangers of mining were all too well known – so much so that the risks of working underground were even used as the subject for popular music hall songs.

Postcard publishers Bamforth & Co. produced series of illustrated song cards with the words of the most popular ones. Several sets of cards with the words of Robert Donnelly and Will Geddes' 1910 song *Don't go Down in the Mine Dad* – the song inspired by the 1907 disaster at St Genard Colliery in South Wales.

For Bamforth's postcards and lantern slides, the title was shortened to *Don't go Down the Mine, Dad.* At least two of the sets were illustrated with a boy as the central figure, the others with a little girl. Several – at least three – different

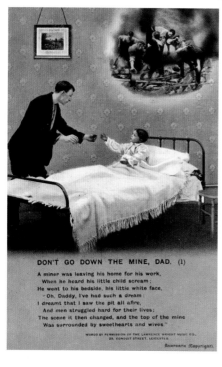

DON'T GO DOWN THE MINE, DAD. (1)

A miner was leaving his home for his work,
When he heard his little child scream;
He went to his bedside, his little white face,
"Oh, Daddy, I've had such a dream;
I dreamt that I saw the pit all afire,
And men struggled hard for their lives;
The scene it then changed, and the top of the mine
Was surrounded by sweethearts and wives."

WORDS BY PERMISSION OF THE LAWRENCE WRIGHT MUSIC CO.,
19, CONDUIT STREET, LEICESTER.

BAMFORTH (Copyright)

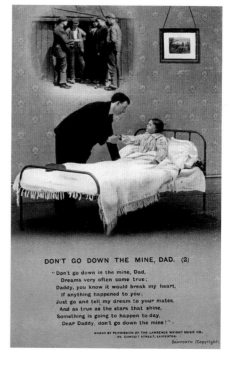

DON'T GO DOWN THE MINE, DAD. (2)

"Don't go down in the mine, Dad,
Dreams very often come true;
Daddy, you know it would break my heart,
If anything happened to you;
Just go and tell my dream to your mates,
And as true as the stars that shine,
Something is going to happen to-day,
Dear Daddy, don't go down the mine!"

WORDS BY PERMISSION OF THE LAWRENCE WRIGHT MUSIC CO.,
19, CONDUIT STREET, LEICESTER.

BAMFORTH (Copyright)

series of inset picture were used on the first three cards in each variant on the set, and four different versions of the final card, each using composite images made up of photographs taken at a number of different collieries.

One version of the set was also available as tinted lantern slides. The tear-jerking chorus ran:

Don't go down in the mine, Dad,
Dreams very often come true;
Daddy, you know it would break my heart
If anything happened to you;
Just go and tell my dream to your mates,
And as true as the stars that shine,
Something is going to happen today,
Dear Daddy, don't go down the mine!

Three further series, *Heroes of the Mine* (see p6) *A Miner's Dream of Home* and *The Collier's Life* (see p34) were also hugely popular. They all used a combination of posed groups and

Below: *Don't go Down in the Mine, Dad,* published by Bamforth in 1910. The Lawrence Wright Music Company had acquired the publishing rights to the song just weeks before the Wellington Pit Disaster in Whitehaven in 1910, and advertised that half the proceeds from the sale of the first 10,000 copies of the sheet music would go to the miners' relief fund. They eventually sold 500,000 copies. The inset image on card No. 1 was used, more vividly coloured for lantern slide No. 4.

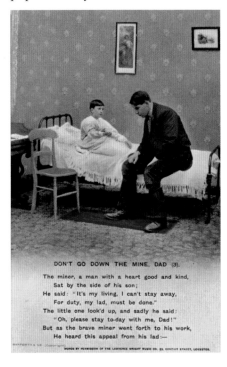

DON'T GO DOWN THE MINE, DAD. (3).

The miner, a man with a heart good and kind,
   Sat by the side of his son;
He said: "It's my living, I can't stay away,
   For duty, my lad, must be done."
The little one look'd up, and sadly he said:
   "Oh, please stay to-day with me, Dad!"
But as the brave miner went forth to his work,
   He heard this appeal from his lad:—

WORDS BY PERMISSION OF THE LAWRENCE WRIGHT MUSIC CO. 24, CONDUIT STREET, LEICESTER.

DON'T GO DOWN THE MINE, DAD. (4)

Whilst waiting his turn with his mates to descend
   He could not banish his fears;
He return'd home again to his wife and his child,
   Those words seem'd to ring through his ears.
And ere the day ended the pit was on fire,
   When a score of brave men lost their lives;
He thank'd God above for the dream his child had,
   As once more the little one cried:—

WORDS BY PERMISSION OF THE LAWRENCE WRIGHT MUSIC CO., 24, CONDUIT STREET, LEICESTER.

BAMFORTH (Copyright.

views of collieries, all overpainted with smoke and flames.

The fear of an explosion was ever-present, the risk heightened by the high concentrations of firedamp found in many British collieries, and the practice of still using naked candle flames to light workplaces underground.

It was normal practice in coalmines, for safety reasons, to withdraw all the miners to the surface before shot-firing – a daily activity to loosen the coal in the years before mechanised cutters became the norm.

This was probably the most dangerous activity in the pit, and records show it was the trigger for a high proportion of mining disasters.

Many British mines were prone to 'firedamp' – a build up of methane gas which, when combined with air, produces a highly inflammable mixture. Firedamp build-up was exacerbated by climate conditions, and so great was the risk at certain times of year, that

DON'T GO DOWN THE MINE, DAD (No. 4).

Whilst waiting his turn with his mates to descend
He could not banish his fears;
He return'd home again to his wife and his child,
Those words seem'd to ring through his ears.
And ere the day ended the pit was on fire.
When a score of brave men lost their lives;
He thank'd God above for the dream his child had,
As once more the little one cried:—

Bamforth (Copyright)
WORDS BY PERMISSION OF THE LAWRENCE WRIGHT MUSIC CO.; 28, CONDUIT STREET, LEICESTER.

DON'T GO DOWN THE MINE, DAD. (3)

The miner, a man with a heart good and kind,
Sat by the side of his son;
He said: "It's my living, I can't stay away,
For duty, my lad, must be done."
The little one look'd up, and sadly he said:
"Oh, please stay to-day with me, Dad!"
But as the brave miner went forth to his work,
He heard this appeal from his lad:—

WORDS BY PERMISSION OF THE LAWRENCE WRIGHT MUSIC CO.,
28, CONDUIT STREET, LEICESTER.
Bamforth (Copyright)

DURHAM MINE DISASTER.
Fire Damp Explosion at the Glebe Colliery, Washington.
14 Miners Crushed and Burnt to Death and One Seriously Injured. Thursday, February 20th, 1908.

Published by W. Gothard, 6, Eldon Street, Barnsley.

national newspapers even carried warnings. *The Times* carried one such warning in August 1908.

The British Coalfields are again covered by an extensive area of high barometric pressure, in which the atmosphere is maintained in a very dry state. Under these circumstances, it is highly desirable that all persons employed in underground workings should pay the closest attention to any indication of the escape of firedamp from the strata, and also see that, in the neighbourhood of blasting operations, the coal-dust is kept in a sufficiently moistened state to render it perfectly safe.

The flash from the dynamite shots being fired was all it took to initiate a chain reaction which was invariably fatal. The methane would ignite, in turn setting alight the coal dust particles in the air, sucking the oxygen out of the atmosphere causing a partial vacuum. This would, in turn, create a powerful wind in the narrow tunnels, and send fireballs rolling through the underground roadways at speeds of 100mph. Nothing in their path could survive. And, despite much lower barometric pressure at the time, that is exactly what happened at the Glebe Colliery in Washington on 20 February 1908.

Above: This card only listed 13 of the men who died at Glebe. Early reports had mistakenly suggested that Thomas Errington had survived.

Opposite: Several of the alternative versions of *Don't go Down the Mine, Dad* used over-painted composites of scenes from other collieries. The tableaux of miners and waiting families were photographed separately and added to the montage.

Gothard of Barnsley's photo-composite of the Hamstead fire – one of a series of at least five different postcards of the disaster – was on sale just two or three days after fire engulfed the mine.

Opposite: Two versions of this card exist, one with no publisher's name, and the other illustrated here. Both versions are believed to have been created by Gothard of Barnsley.

Glebe was a new colliery owned by the Washington Coal Company, its 720ft shaft sunk in 1901-2, the mine opened in 1904, and the first coal was cut in 1905.

Then on that fateful Monday evening in February 1908, disaster struck. Only fifteen men were working in the lowest seam preparing and firing the shots; only one survived the conflagration. The first detailed report of the disaster appeared in *The Times* two days later.

It was just about 10 o'clock when the first intimation of disaster was heard at the bank. There was a loud explosion, followed by a rumbling which was heard all over the populous district round about the pit. So strong, indeed, was the shock at the pit mouth that the "waiting on" man at the top of the shaft was knocked over on to his back. At once he sent for the deputy, a man named Ingleby, who in turn informed Mr. Ford, the manager, of the calamity. Mr. Ford, accompanied by Ingleby and some ten men, formed the first party to descend the mine. The men in the two higher seams had heard the sound of the explosion, and had all succeeded in getting safely out of the pit without mishap, and it was only in the low main seam that any one remained to be looked for. Here there were 15 men at work. Arriving at the bottom of the shaft, the rescue party found all round them extensive indications of the force of the explosion. The timbering was blown down in all directions, and all over the seam there were falls of stone and roof, brought away by the force of the blast.

First to meet the rescuers' view was the pump man, a man named Yeardsley, whom they found badly injured crawling towards the shaft bottom. He was at once attended to. The air at this time was very bad owing to the prevalence of after-damp in the seam. Six times did the rescue party endeavour to force their way into the seam ; six times they were repulsed, and forced to wait till the air cleared sufficiently to enable them to penetrate.

The disaster left fourteen families fatherless, and in those days, there was little in the way of financial support for the widows and children. Selling postcards was one of the ways of raising a small sum of money, and commemorative postcards bearing the faces of the dead became a common feature of Edwardian mining disasters.

Just two weeks later on 4 March, at the Hamstead Colliery in Great Barr, Birmingham, an underground fire claimed the lives of twenty-five miners and one member of the rescue team. The youngest, Joseph Hodgkiss, a time-keeper on the night shift, was just seventeen years old.

This postcard, produced by local publishers, Scotts, shows men hard at work trying to lay pipes to improve ventilation to the burning mine in an effort to aid recovery of those still trapped below. The mine had very quickly filled with thick acrid smoke, and 25 were already dead.

The Hamstead Colliery Disaster.

Problems at the colliery had started two days earlier when the winding engine on the main shaft broke down, leaving only one winding engine, on the No. 2 shaft, operational. That fact would play a significant role in the eventual loss of life.

With only one working shaft – official regulations required that there be two – getting men out of the mine took much longer than it should have. Mining should, in fact, have been suspended until the main winding engine had been repaired and was operational again.

Smoke was first noticed about 5.15pm, near the office at the foot of the shaft, and the first several attempts to descend to the pit bottom were abandoned due to the density of the smoke.

By the time rescuers got within a few feet of the shaft bottom, they

reported that they could hear the rumble of roofs collapsing between the two shafts. There had only been twenty five men working below ground at the time, and all perished.

A crowd estimated at 8,000 people soon gathered outside the pityard to await news – a scene repeated after colliery disasters across the country. At Great Barr, their grief was intensified by an unfortunate coincidence long before the outcome of the rescue attempts was known.

The pit's under-manager, Joseph Hughes had been killed underground on 28 February, and his funeral had been arranged – setting out from the colliery yard – for 4 March. The wreath-laden cortege of shining black coaches drew up in front of the crowd at the pit gates, just as the rescue team prepared to go underground!

Several postcard companies – including Gothards – quickly published cards to commemorate the loss of life, and in addition to the general views of the devastated pithead surrounded by cameo portraits of the dead, two of the Gothard series had a much more personal resonance. The

Amongst the most emotionally charged of Gothard's cards are two from the Hamstead disaster – one dedicated to John Welsby, the rescuer who lost his life (*above*) and the other (*above left*) showing 'three brothers named Johnson' waiting for their brother's body to be brought out.

brothers Johnson waiting for their dead brother's body to be brought to the surface was one, but perhaps even more heart-wrenching, one of the cards commemorated the member of the rescue team, John Welsby, who also lost his life. Gothards, however, were by no means alone in wishing to commemorate Welsby's heroism.

An unidentified local photographer produced an extensive series of cards illustrating and commemorating his funeral – an event which brought thousands on to the streets to line the route as the cortege passed, and underlined the very deep-felt gratitude any mining community felt for those willing to put their own lives at risk in order to try and rescue others.

The story of John Welsby's funeral was told in a series of postcards, published locally in West Yorkshire, photographer unknown.

As with every major disaster, the rescue teams came from far and wide, and Welsby was a member of the Altofts Rescue Team from a mining village near Wakefield in West Yorkshire.

112

Perhaps that is one of the reason his death was given such prominence by Gothards, themselves based in Yorkshire.

Welsby quickly became known as the 'Altofts Hero' – but interestingly several of the postcards refer to the village as 'Altoft', and to him as 'Altoft's Hero'!

But, thus, he stood apart from the other victims of the disaster, as the only one who was not local to the Great Barr area, and the only casualty to die far away from home.

Circulation of the postcards of Welsby's funeral, produced as they almost certainly were by a local photographer, was probably limited only to the immediate area of his home village – postcard-size photographic printing paper was widely available by that time with the standard format of a postcard back already pre-printed, so it is likely that the production run for these very rare cards was small. None of the examples seen of these cards has been postally used, their purchasers collecting them as mementoes to be treasured in family postcard albums. In that respect, they really serve as news pictures.

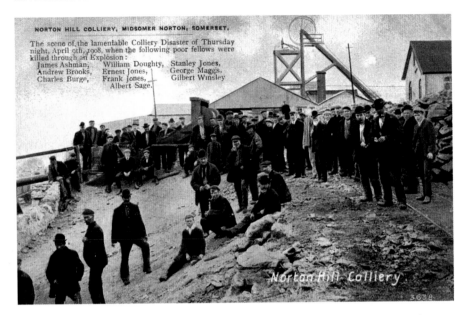

NORTON HILL COLLIERY, MIDSOMER NORTON, SOMERSET.

The scene of the lamentable Colliery Disaster of Thursday night, April 9th, 1908, when the following poor fellows were killed through an Explosion:
James Ashman, William Doughty, Stanley Jones,
Andrew Brooks, Ernest Jones, George Maggs,
Charles Burge, Frank Jones, Gilbert Winsley
Albert Sage.

To date, this view of the pityard at Norton Hill is the only disaster card yet found to have been printed in colour. The sombre quality of monochrome was usually deemed to be the appropriate form in which to commemorate those who had lost their lives.

Heroism was a recurring feature of the mining industry, and thus of the newspaper reporting of every accident, and many postcard publishers did the same thing. On the back of a postcard of men waiting for news at the pithead of Norton Hill Colliery, Midsomer Norton, in the Somerset coalfield in 1908, we read,

On Thursday night, April 9th 1908, this pit was the scene of a calamity which filled the district with sorrow and horror. Between 9 and 10 o'clock when the night shift had been down about an hour, it is supposed that the coal dust was ignited by blasting, and ten of the workers were added to the roll of victims of Colliery disasters, most of them being literally hurled into eternity, other having apparently succumbed to afterdamp. It was an unspeakable mercy that the explosion did not happen during the day when so many more men would have been in the mine, with relatively more terrible results. The gloom is lightened by the knowledge of the heroism displayed by the rescuers who nobly hastened to the work of rescue and had in several cases to be themselves saved, their fellow helpers finding them insensible in the workings. Dr Pollard and Dr Miall both descended the shaft and rendered all possible assistance.

The most ambitious of Gothard's disaster cards managed to gather together portraits of 117 of the 168 men who lost their lives in the West Stanley explosion in 1909. As many of the miners had rarely been photographed – many of them not since childhood – a number of the faces which stare out from this poignant card look much too young to ever have been allowed to venture underground.

Ten men died in the disaster. What is remarkable about so many of these cards is the speed of their production. The card (*opposite*) is a particularly interesting example. The scene it depicts must have been photographed on the morning of 10 April, the day after the explosion. The card, which was posted in Midsomer Norton, carries a postmark date of 11 April, probably the date it was published, just 24 hours after the photograph was taken, and 36 hours after the disaster.

Coal mining has always been a dangerous undertaking, and over the centuries, thousands of lives have been lost in British mines to keep the wheels of industry turning.

Throughout the Victorian and Edwardian eras, the annual number of deaths rose significantly. It peaked in 1910 at 1,818! Of several major explosions in that year, the 344 deaths at Westoughton's Pretoria Pit was the worst in almost fifty years, since 388 men died at the Oaks Colliery in Barnsley in 1866.

Even that would be eclipsed before the outbreak of the Great War, when Britain's worst-ever mining disaster – the explosion at the Universal Colliery in Senghenydd, Glamorgan – took 439 lives. 81 men had died in the same colliery on 24 May 1901.

Perhaps because of the numbers employed, the death toll in the Welsh coalfields in the nineteenth century had been notoriously high. The Edwardian years were a little less expensive in terms of human life despite the toll at Senghenydd in 1901, and the 119 who died at Wattstown in Glamorgan, in July 1905. Since 1850, over 100,000 miners have died in British pits.

This card, published by Gothard and wholesaled by W. H. Smith, shows the thirty survivors from the West Stanley Colliery explosion.

Until the dawn of the twentieth century, most of the 1000+ deaths each year were marked by no more than a few lines in a local newspaper or, if the disaster was on a large enough scale, in the national press. Most went completely unreported, save for the required note in the colliery records. But of those deaths which did warrant a published account, some of the stories can still tug at the heartstrings more than a century later; others describe the scene so graphically that pictures were probably unnecessary.

In the early weeks of 1882, a young woman from Trimdon near Sedgefield, County Durham, was looking forward to her wedding. She was to marry a miner who worked at the coal-face in Trimdon Grange Colliery.

The wedding was to take place on Saturday 25 February 1882, but the day turned out to be very different from her plans. Yes, she was in church at the appointed time – but not to be married. Instead she attended her fiancé's funeral – he had been killed nine days earlier in the explosion which ripped through the mine and took seventy-four lives. Sad to say, colliery records across the country all tell of the huge price miners have paid ever since deep mining began in Britain four centuries ago.

Waiting for news – the scene in the Maypole Colliery yard on the evening of 18 August 1908. Smoke can clearly be seen billowing around the partially demolished fan house and the head-gear for the No.1 shaft. By the time this photograph was taken, the local police had thrown a cordon around the devastated pit buildings, keeping the growing crowd at a distance so as not to impede the rescue teams as they went about their work.

117

Below: Within just a few days of the Maypole disaster, local postcard publisher Will Smith had produced this postcard of the only three men to survive the blast. It was probably photographed in Millard's Wigan studio. The three men became minor local celebrities, with this same photograph being published in the *Wigan Observer*.

Bottom: Crowds gather in the pityard just hours after the explosion at the Maypole Colliery.

Like any mining area, the North East of England had its fair share of explosions. Writing in his book *A Tour Thro' the Whole Island of Great Britain* in the late 1720s, Daniel Defoe, of *Robinson Crusoe* fame, gave a graphic account of one which took place in 1727.

Here we had an account of a melancholy accident and in itself strange also, which happened in or near Lumley Park, not long before we pass'd through the town. A new coal pit being dug, the workmen work on in the vein of coals till they came to a cavity, which, as was supposed, had formerly been dug from some other pit; but be it what it will, as soon as upon the breaking into the hollow part, the pent up air got vent, it blew up like a mine of a thousand barrels of powder, and getting vent at the shaft of the pit, burst out with such a terrible noise, as made the very earth tremble for some miles round, and terrify'd the whole country.

There were near three-score poor people lost their lives in the pit, and one or two, as we were told, who were at the bottom of the shaft, were blown quite out, though sixty fathom deep, and

THE ONLY
SURVIVORS
OF THE
DISASTER
AT THE
MAYPOLE
COLLIERY,
ABRAM.
AUGUST 18TH, 1908.

EDWARD FARRELL, 3, CAMBRIDGE ST., WIGAN.   WM. DORAN, 6, HARDYBUTTS, WIGAN.   RICHARD FAIRHURST, 11, CROWN STREET, HINDLEY.

Will Smith series, Wigan. Copyright.

AUG 18th 1908. No 2.
MAYPOLE COLLIERY DISASTER. WAITING FOR NEWS.

118

were found dead upon the ground. [Between 1727 and 1827, over 150 men lost their lives at that pit.]

On the other side of the country, and more than 180 years later, a postcard sent by Charles Holmes – who came from Otley in Yorkshire, but worked in Lancashire – tells of the worst disaster in the Wigan coalfield, at the Maypole Colliery in Abram, operated by the Moss Hall Coal Company Ltd. He wrote to his sister Jennie on 28 August 1908,

My Dear Sister, I am coming home tomorrow by the 8.55 train from Bradford. How would you have liked being 200 feet up in the air with me yesterday? We had a splendid view of the country around. Tell Pa I am quite safe so he need not feel anxious. I wrote this pc. while on the top.

"On the top" may well have meant 'in the pit yard', as this was a common expression at the time. That is perhaps reinforced by Charles's 'ps' in which he remarks that "The fire is still raging at the Maypole Pit here, it has burned the cage gearing down." That was ten days after the mining community heard the rumble of the explosion deep underground, and

Above: This Gothard card featured the Maypole rescuers, and the two types of breathing apparatus they used – Draeger and WEG. The WEG equipment had been designed by William E. Garforth.

Overleaf: On a James Starr card, possibly in Wigan's Junction Pit – through which the Maypole survivors escaped – is a rare message from an eyewitness.

...tion in a coal mine.

A little more than two years after their heroic efforts in Abram, three members of the Maypole rescue team, J. Robinson, J. Touhey and R. Picton prepare to go down into the Hulton Colliery Company's No. 3 pit at Westhoughton – the Pretoria – after the explosion there. The caption to this scene reads 'A Party of Maypole Rescue Team – Going to help the imprisoned miners at the Pretoria Colliery Disaster, December 21st 1910'.

knew their ever-present fears were now reality, and eight days after attempts to extinguish the fire by partially flooding the mine had been instigated. Work to flood the mine had been started on the night of Thursday 20 August.

The postcard Holmes used was an unusual one – but appropriate. It showed a trackway junction deep underground, taken some years earlier by professional photographer Thomas Taylor. It may even be the point where Junction Colliery's underground railway met the Maypole's. The two pits shared many seams and roadways, and indeed, the fan-house destroyed at the Maypole supplied supplementary air to the Junction Colliery's workings.

Thomas Taylor was a regular visitor to local collieries, and had been producing and marketing views of the collieries in the Wigan coalfield since the early 1890s.

Indeed, it was to his earlier pioneering underground views of the collieries – taken in the closing decade of the nineteenth century – that local postcard publishers turned in 1905, converting his sepia images into beautifully tinted postcards. By the time Charles actually posted his card to Jennie, Taylor would have spent some of the previous week and more photographing the destruction in the pit yard. His photographs of the disaster were published in local newspapers, and much further afield.

To find a postcard or a letter from an eye-witness, or perhaps even a participant, really brings the story of any event into sharp focus. The story becomes human rather than just an historical fact, and a first-hand experience rather than a secondhand account.

To find a postcard apparently written from the site of a disaster is rare indeed!

The explosion took place just after 5pm – just over an hour after the day shift had returned to the surface, leaving the underground roadways to the maintenance men, the men who manned the pumps, those who tended to the needs of the ponies, and to the firemen – the shot-firers who set charges to blast the coal which would be hewn and brought to the surface the following day.

William Doran, one of the three survivors, later told *The Times* newspaper about the actual moment of the explosion.

> *I was knocked down by the force of the explosion and fell face forward. We tried to travel along the road towards the pit eye, but all the lights went out except one and we were afraid to go on. We decided to await events in a manhole.*

There they remained for some hours before a rescue party reached them, and led them to safety and back to the surface via one of the shafts of the nearby Junction Colliery. Twenty-four hours later, another of the three, Richard Fairhurst, fully

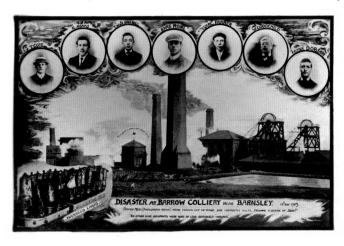

Disaster at Barrow Colliery, near Barnsley, 15 November 1907.

recovered from the ordeal, posed for a photograph with his wife and baby daughter. A total of 75 men had not been so lucky.

Had the crowds who quickly gathered around the pityard known just where the explosion had taken place – nearly three thousand feet below ground and two thirds of a mile

from the bottom of the shaft – then the devastation to the fan-house and adjacent buildings would have left them little hope of there being any survivors. The blast had travelled more than a mile and a half along the roadways and up the shaft itself, and yet still had sufficient power to lift the fan-house roof completely off!

Opposite page: These Gothard postcards of the Maypole explosion in August 1908 claimed 76 dead – but actually listed 77 – and claimed 7 survivors. In fact, the death toll was 75 – one man, William Moore had lost his tally and not reported the fact. Another, George Melling disappeared for three days, and by the time he reappeared, his family had provided a photograph of him, and the first of Gothard's card was already on sale. Only three survived. The original card, (opposite top) which included portraits of 27 of the victims, was withdrawn from sale after a few days, and replaced by a second version (opposite below) which included portraits of an additional four men. By that time, Moore and Melling were both known to have survived, but, perhaps surprisingly, both were still listed amongst the dead.

This page: The Maypole eventually ceased production in 1962. The brick base of the No. 2 shaft headgear remained until demolished early this century.

In the days immediately after the disaster, a surprisingly large number of postcards were published – including the four by Gothard included in this book – and sold widely to help the widows and children.

As was the Barnsley company's practice by that time, two of the Gothard cards included portraits of many of the men who had lost their lives – the photographs all supplied by their families – and even included a photograph of one man believed dead who was, in fact, very much alive!

The Maypole disaster was extensively covered by photographers, and research carried out at the time of the 75th anniversary identified nearly one hundred pictures of the ruined mine, the crowds, the rescuers, and the victims.

Even the victims' funerals were photographed for postcards to raise money for the bereaved in the days before welfare payments.

Major national postcard publishers like Valentines produced several cards showing funerals, the wrecked pithead, and general scenes of despair and anxiety.

Newspapers, of course, rarely included photographs in those days, so these cards served an important information role, as well as contributing to the welfare fund. The majority of them were published days before the local newspaper, the *Wigan Observer*, published its illustrated account of the disaster.

But even the extensive postcard coverage of the Maypole pales when compared with the series of cards which chronicled

Like most collieries, the pithead buildings at the Maypole have all now disappeared. The pithead buildings were demolished in 2004. This housing estate, built two years later, stands on the site of of the pityard, scene of the 1908 explosion. Only a replica coal truck pays tribute to the site's mining past. A service in 2008 was held to mark the centenary of the disaster.

and commemorated Europe's worst ever mining disaster which occurred at Courrères in Northern France early in the morning of 10 March 1906. In the fires which followed a dust explosion deep underground in a mine operated by the Compagnie des mines de houille de Courrières just to the east of Lens, 1099 men and boys died. The adult male population of the four nearest villages was decimated.

There had been more than 1500 men working underground at the time of the explosion, and more than two thirds of them had been killed.

For a disaster on such an unexpected scale, a large number of postcards were produced, and sold in considerable numbers.

From scenes of the mine itself, to almost journalistic sequences of cards telling the stories of the rescue, through to the funerals and burials of the victims, the postcard photographers were never far away. Everything was covered from the crowds waiting for news, through to the remarkable story of 13 survivors who became known as 'les escapés' after they were found underground on 30 March, 20 days after the original blast.

They had survived by eating food from the lunch boxes taken underground by those of their colleagues who had died, and eventually by eating one of the pit ponies! Three of

Valentine of Dundee published several series of commemorative mining cards. This shows the funeral of Thomas Henry Pimblett, one of the victims of the Maypole explosion. Pimblett lived opposite the end of Park Lane in Abram – the road which led down to the Maypole Colliery.

Equipe de *Sauveteurs* Français et Allemands en tenue de travail.
Un de ces Sauveteurs est mort victime de son dévouement.

Cliché Favère, éditeur, Lens.   Reproduction interdite.

Above: French and German rescuers pose with their equipment before venturing into the Courrières mine. At the time, mine rescue teams were few and far between in France, and additional experts were brought in from Germany. The first of those teams arrived on 12 March 1906.

Right: A body is brought out of the mine, past mine officials and a photographer adjusting his camera.

them were just boys – still permitted to work underground in French pits. A final survivor was discovered on 5 April, having managed to keep himself alive for just two days short of four weeks!

The idea of producing or sending a postcard to commemorate a disaster may seem odd today, but to those who lived in the early years of last century, with no tele-

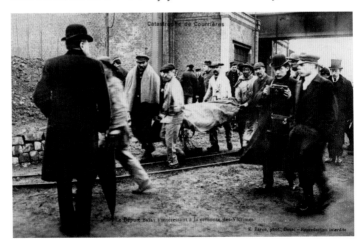

128

phones, illustrated newspapers, radio or television, how else could pictures of important stories be disseminated?

Perhaps surprisingly, the Pretoria disaster in 1910, where more than three hundred miners lost their lives, was not the subject of anything like as many postcards. But by then, of course, photographic illustrations in newspapers were much more commonplace, albeit at a quality far below that which could be achieved by the postcard publishers – who were, of course, usually printing on to quality card rather than newsprint.

The research for this book has failed to reveal any postcards commemorating accidents in the Scottish coalfield, yet there was frequent loss of life albeit, thankfully, not on the scale of the major disasters south of the border.

The only records discovered thus far are newspaper accounts of lives lost. Both of the major daily newspapers – the *Scotsman* and the *Glasgow Herald* – reported mining accidents. From the *Scotsman* of 15 June 1904 we read

Despite the blizzard, huge crowds turned out for the funerals, and postcards told every stage of the story at the Courrières mine.

The thirteen Courrières survivors brought out of the mine after 20 days underground pose for the camera with Dr Lourties who had tended to the injured when they were brought to the surface. Given that many of those brought out in the early days following the explosion had, according to the Dr Lourties, died of pneumonia within 50 to 60 hours of rescue, the survival of the 13 'escapés' is remarkable.

Early yesterday morning a serious accident occurred at Allanshaw Colliery, Hamilton, resulting in shocking burning injuries to Patrick Harrison, miner, and the death of his son Thomas. Early in the morning a dull noise was heard by a man at the pit bottom. This circumstance he communicated to one of the colliery officials, with the result that a search was made, when the younger Harrison was found dead and the father unconscious and in a precarious condition. There is said to be evidence of an explosion, but the remarkable circumstance is that the workings are uninjured, and the safety lamps of both men were found locked. The elder Harrison was removed to the Royal Infirmary in the ambulance waggon, and faint hope is entertained of his recovery.

That faint hope was, however, sadly misplaced, and the next day the paper reported

The Allanshaw Colliery Accident – Patrick Harrison, miner, Hamilton, who, along with his son, was severely burned in Allanshaw Colliery on Tuesday morning, and who was removed to the Glasgow Royal Infirmary, died yesterday.

During the Edwardian era, 24 miners lost their lives in the collieries around Hamilton and Blantyre alone, and while some of them were reported in detail, others just got short mention. One of the more detailed accounts comes from the *Scotsman* which reported an accident at No. 8 pit Quarter Colliery, Hamilton, just a few days before Christmas 1906.

Fatal Colliery Accident At Quarter – Yesterday afternoon a serious colliery accident which resulted in the loss of three lives took place in No. 8 pit Quarter Colliery belonging to the United Collieries (Limited.). Full information is not yet to hand but it appears that about two o'clock the engineman in the winding house felt a grip on the tow rope as the cage was going down the shaft, indicating that something was amiss in the shaft; and confirmation was given to this by a piece of the slide on which the cage runs falling to the pit bottom. The manager Mr Robert Gardiner assisted by the overman Andrew Maxwell and James MacGinty, then proceeded up the shaft to make an examination. They had ascended some distance when a mass of material – stones and dirt – came away from the side above them and broke the tow rope. The result was that the cage and the men were precipitated to the pit bottom. The cage was crushed almost flat, while

THE ONLY SURVIVORS
From the PRETORIA PIT DISASTER, WESTHOUGHTON, December 21st, 1910, in which 344 lives were lost.
Amount Collected for the BOLTON MAYOR'S RELIEF FUND—£88,440.
Copyright by C. W. Lloyd, Taxidermist, who has received an acknowledgment from the King and Queen.

HULTON PIT DISASTER

Above: Despite the fact that a large number of miners escaped the pit unhurt, only these three were celebrated as 'survivors'.

Left: The scene in the pityard shortly after the Pretoria disaster in 1910.

the men's bodies were covered with a huge mass of wreckage and rubbish. Death must have been instantaneous.

The pit is very deep, one shaft going down something like one hundred and fifty fathoms. A relief party was at once formed under the charge of Mr MacDougall manager of Upper Quarter pits, and Mr Arnott district manager for the company arrived on the scene, while Drs. Steel and Stewart were in early attendance with the view of rendering any possible assistance. It was quickly ascertained however that hope for the survival of any of the men was out of the question. Strenuous efforts were made to have the bodies unearthed but at nine o'clock, when our representative left, they had not been recovered though they were momentarily expected at the pithead. About two hundred miners were at work when the accident happened but they were brought to the surface by No.7 pit which adjoins No.8.

News of the calamity quickly spread to the village and naturally there was great excitement and grief. Large crowds gathered about the pithead where arrangements had been made for coffining the bodies as soon as they were brought up. All three men were well up in years, and leave widows and large families, MacGinty leaving nine children.

Quarter village is situated about three miles from Hamilton. Coal has been worked from the Quarter field from an early period but No. 8 pit was only sunk twenty years ago

December 1907 was an especially bad month for the mining industry in the United States. On 6 December at the Monongah Mine of the Fairmont Coal Company, 361 of the 366 men working underground were killed in a dust explosion. Amongst the fatalities was an insurance salesman who had actually been selling insurance underground to the men. Less than two weeks later, on 19 December, a gas and dust explosion at the Darr Mine cost another 239 lives. Amongst the rare tinted postcards commemorating the disaster was this scene of open coffins inside a marquee set up as a temporary morgue, the bodies awaiting identification.

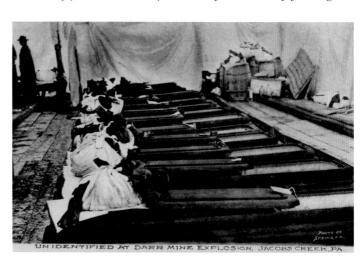

UNIDENTIFIED AT DARR MINE EXPLOSION, JACOBS CREEK, PA.

The buildings at Whitehaven's Wellington Colliery were given battlements and turrets to make it look like a coastal castle. This postcard dates from 1904. The underground explosion at this pit on 11 May 1910 cost 136 lives.

for the purpose of winning Simpsonland coalfield. The collieries were formerly owned by Messrs Colin Dunlop & Company but they were taken over by the United Collieries at the time of the flotation of that company. This is the first accident on a large scale that has taken place at Quarter.

Postcards of Scottish collieries are, themselves, surprisingly scarce, so perhaps there was just not the market for them, despite a large percentage of Scotland's population living in the central belt. Or was there was just a reluctance amongst miners and their families to encourage publishers to produce such cards? In any event, newspaper reports of Scottish mining disasters were shocking enough.

By the early years of the First World War, with photographs increasingly being published in daily newspapers – albeit at a much lower quality than had become the norm with postcards – demand for 'disaster' cards in general rapidly fell away. After the Minnie Pit disaster at Halmers End in Staffordshire in January 1915, in which 155 men lost their lives, even Gothards ceased production of them.

Not all the postcards of Edwardian mining disasters concentrated on the disasters themselves. Amongst the more unusual and poignant of the postcards reproduced a message of sympathy sent from Queen Alexandra to the Mayor of Whitehaven after the 11 May explosion at the Wellington Colliery in Whitehaven at which 136 men lost their lives.

Alexandra, herself recently bereaved and getting used to being Queen Mother rather than Queen, was sufficiently moved by the disaster to express her feelings publicly.

The explosion deep underground was probably triggered by a faulty miner's lamp, and, in the presence of both coal dust and large pockets of methane, disaster would have been inevitable.

Despite the best efforts of several rescue teams, the decision was eventually made to seal the mine, but not everyone believed at the time that sufficient effort had been made to save the men and boys below ground – the youngest of whom was just 15 years old.

Local concerns and doubts persisted, and the matter was even raised in the House of Commons, by the labour politician Keir Hardie who berated the then Home Secretary, Winston Churchill, with a powerful and provocative indictment:

Queen Alexandra's message of condolence to the widows and families of the Whitehaven victims was published as a postcard by A. & G. Taylor of London who, in Victorian times, had operated a photographic studio in almost every large town in England.

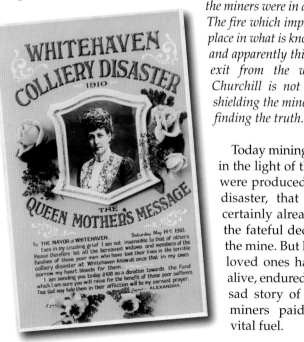

I give it as my opinion, based upon my practical experience as a miner, that at the time it was decided to wall up the mine, the miners were in all probability, still alive. The fire which imprisoned the miners, took place in what is known as "The Bottleneck" and apparently this was the only means of exit from the workings…I hope Mr. Churchill is not more concerned about shielding the mine owner than he is about finding the truth.

Today mining experts generally agree, in the light of the official reports which were produced in the aftermath of the disaster, that the men were almost certainly already all dead long before the fateful decision was taken to seal the mine. But locally, the fear that their loved ones had, in fact, been buried alive, endured for many years, another sad story of the heavy price which miners paid to produce Britain's vital fuel.

An unusual memento of the Maypole disaster in August 1908, a decorated napkin bearing the names of the miners who had died. Napkins were produced to commemorate the dead from several Lancashire disasters, including the Pretoria. The black overprinting of the names of the dead was simply printed over existing commercially produced paper napkins, so examples survive with several different flower motif borders.

There were, of course, many other mementoes produced to commemorate those who lost their lives in mining disasters – amongst them poems, printed paper napkins, plaques and memorials, but it is the huge number of photographic postcards, a vast visual legacy still being discovered, which really tells the miners' story in a tangible way.

Within two years of the end of the Edwardian era, the 1912 National Colliery Strike brought all the nation's pits to a standstill for five weeks. The following year, after the worst disaster of them all, when 439 men died at the Universal Colliery in Senghenydd, Glamorgan on 4 October 1913, many postcards were published to raise money for the Disaster Fund The following year Britain was at war, and coal output reached it peak.

The postcard industry never quite returned to its huge diversity of output after the war, with illustrated newspapers taking on much of the role which the local 'disaster' cards had filled just a decade earlier.

The head frame at the
Lady Victoria Colliery,
Scottish Mining
Museum were built
by William Arrol &
Company who also
built the Forth Bridge.

COAL MINING MUSEUMS

Big Pit: National Coal Museum Wales
www.museumwales.ac.uk/en/bigpit   tel: 029 2057 3650   Blaenafon, Torfaen, NP4 9XP
A key part of the impressive and important Blaenafon World Heritage Site, and with some buildings dating back to the 1870s, the museum offers a living history of Welsh coal mining. Highlight of a visit is the underground tour, 300ft below ground, with a 50-minute guided walk around the coal face, stables and engine houses. Visitors wear the very same equipment – helmet, cap lamp, belt, battery and 'self rescuer' – formerly used by the miners. Admission is free, paying only for car parking.

National Coal Mining Museum for England
www.ncm.org.uk   tel: 01924 848806
Caphouse Colliery, New Road, Overton, Wakefield, WF4 4RH
Set on a huge 17 acre site, the museum includes the Hope Pit, lamp room, furnace shaft, an 1876 steam winder, and an underground tour 400ft below ground. Visitors also see the pithead baths, now home to permanent and temporary exhibitions. The Coal Interface Gallery allows visitors to see how machinery was used to hew the coal, while Mining Lives focuses on a miner's home and leisure life. Admission is free.

National Mining Museum Scotland
www.scottishminingmuseum.com   tel: 0131 663 7519
Lady Victoria Colliery, Newtongrange, Midlothian, EH22 4QN
As a consequence of being mothballed for several years by the National Coal Board after production ceased in 1981, the Lady Victoria Colliery, which opened in 1895, is the most complete survival of a Victorian and Edwardian coalmining complex in Europe. The four-acre Midlothian site very effectively captures the developments in mining over generations and highlights include the most powerful steam winding engine in Scotland, the most extensive preserved suite of Lancashire Boilers in the UK, and the only extant timber Dredger in Europe. There is an admission charge, but free car parking.

Astley Green Colliery Museum
www.agcm.org.uk   tel: 01942 708969
Higher Green Lane, Astley Green, Tyldesley, Manchester M29 7JB
The Astley Green Colliery Museum is run by the Red Rose Steam Society in Astley near Tyldesley in Greater Manchester, incorporating the former Astley Green Colliery. Amongst the exhibits housed in the Engine House is the largest steam winding engine ever used in the Lancashire Coalfield – the 3,300 hp twin tandem compound engine was built by Yates & Thom in 1912. The museum also houses the largest collection of colliery locomotives in the United Kingdom. The existing 400 metres of line, running through the site, is currently used for freight demonstrations. Open Sunday, Tuesday & Thursday pm.

Beamish Open Air Musem
www.beamish.org.uk   tel: 0191 370 4000
Beamish Museum, Beamish, County Durham, DH9 0RG
The vertical winding engine from Beamish 2nd Pit, built in 1855 in Newcastle, is the sole survivor of a type once common in the North East. It is steamed daily in the summer season. The pit yard

is well worth a visit, and amongst the surviving buildings is the colliery lamp room. For special events please see website.

Black Country Living Museum
www.bclm.co.uk   tel: 0121 520 8054   Tipton Road, Dudley DY1 4SQ
A coal mine has been recreated in this massive museum of Black Country life, which covers 26 acres and also features a canal-side village, vintage trams, and a number of other industrial sites. 'Into the Thick' is the museum's underground experience which recreates how miners worked the 'Thick Coal' and other seams in the Black Country in the 1850s. The drift mine with its sloping tunnel leads into a maze of roadways and working areas so visitors can experience something of the underground conditions a century and a half ago. Open daily April to October, and Wednesday to Sunday at other times.

Cefn Coed Colliery Museum
www.npt.gov.uk   tel: 01639 750556   Neath Road, Creunant, SA10 8SN
Cefn Coed Colliery Museum tells the story of coal mining at Cefn Coed pit, once the deepest anthracite coal mine in the world. Cefn Coed was one of the most dangerous coalmines in Wales, gaining the nickname 'The Slaughterhouse'. The museum tells the story – through words, pictures and artefacts – of the thousands of men who worked at Cefn Coed and at other pits in the anthracite coalmines of South West Wales.

Haig Colliery Mining Museum
www.visitcumbria.com/wc/haig-colliery-mining-museum.htm
tel: 01946 599949   Solway Road, Kells, Whitehaven, Cumbria CA28 9BG
The remains of Cumbria's last deep mine which closed in 1986. The winding house has been undergoing restoration since early in 1994 by a group of local volunteers. When the pit closed, many of the buildings were demolished, and the area landscaped to form the Haig Enterprise Park. Only the winding engine house and headgear remained. The building is being restored to its former glory, along with two unique Bever-Dorling steam winding engines.

Hopewell Colliery Museum
No website details   tel: 01594 810706
Speech House Road, Coleford, Gloucestershire, GL16 7EL
Hopewell was opened in 1823 and has used at least three different 'adits' (drifts). It had been closed by the time the Hilton Bros. took it over in 1965. At the time of their retirement (1989) it had been closed and reopened several times. It was bought by Free Miner Robin Morgan in 1992, who converted certain parts into a museum which opened in 1997. The mine still operates in the winter months, and opens as a museum in the summer. Open March to October daily 10am to 4pm.

Tub Circuit, Lady Victoria Colliery. Coal tubs were moved along a narrow gauge railway system – most of it by gravity – to be weighed, and then transported to the shaker screens.

Ironbridge Gorge Museum
www.ironbridge.org.uk   tel: 01952 435900
Coach Rd, Coalbrookdale, Shropshire TF8 7DQ
The industrial heritage complex which makes up the Ironbridge Gorge Museum includes ten museums, and everything from the world's oldest iron bridge to the history of Coalport china. At Blists Hill Victorian town, there is a recreation of a coal mine, a steam lifting engine, and a small pit headgear. Of especial interest, and sited near the Coaport China Museum, the eighteenth century Tar Tunnel has survived from when miners in 1787 located a seam of natural bitumen, which still seeps through the wall two centuries later.

Museum of Cannock Chase
www.wlct.org/Cannock%20Services/Museum/about-your-museum.htm
tel: 01543 877666   Valley Road, Hednesford, Staffordshire WS12 1TD
The museum site was once home to the Valley Colliery, the training pit for thousands of young men beginning their working lives in the local coal industry. The pit has gone and in its place are over 30 acres of green space on the edge of Cannock Chase, at the gateway to the Hednesford Hills Nature Reserve. The museum includes the Miners Cottage Gallery, and the Coal Mining Gallery with crawl through tunnel.

South Wales Miners Museum
www.thevalleys.co.uk/attractions/south-wales-miners-museum   tel: 01639 850 564
Afan Forest Park, Cynonville, Port Talbot, Neath, Port Talbot SA13 3HG
The Welsh Miners' Museum in the Afan Argoed Country Park offers an historical journey back in time through the eyes of the miners themselves. Amongst many exhibits, the museum contains historic photographs, documents and early mining equipment. The museum has also recreated a traditional Miner's Cottage. Open daily Easter to October, winter opening Tuesday to Sunday. Admission charge.

Washington 'F' Pit Museum
www.twmuseums.org.uk/washington.html   tel: 0191 553 2323
Albany Way, Washington, NE37 1BJ
Originally sunk in 1777, by 1870, 'F' Pit had become the largest coal-producing pit at the colliery. It ceased production in 1968. The winding house and headgear were presented by the National Coal Board to the people of Washington and remain today as a tribute to the miners and their work. Admission to Washington 'F' Pit is free and the site is open seasonally. The impressive winding engine is now operated by electricity.

Woodhorn Museum and Northumberland Archives
www.experiencewoodhorn.com   tel: 01670 624455
Queen Elizabeth II Country Park, Ashington, Northumberland, NE63 9YF
Coal mining at Woodhorn ended in 1981 after 83 years, but the shafts continued to be used to service nearby Ashington Colliery until 1986. Since then the site has been developed as the county archives and an interactive museum. The listed buildings are said to be the finest surviving example of a late nineteenth/early twentieth century colliery in the North East.

OTHER MINING MUSEUMS

Cleveland Ironstone Museum
www.ironstonemuseum.co.uk tel: 01287 642877
Deepdale, Skinningrove, Saltburn-by-the-Sea, TS13 4AP
Cleveland Ironstone Mining Museum offers visitors the opportunity to experience the underground world of a real ironstone mine and to explore the skills, customs and life of the Cleveland miner. It was those miners that helped to make Cleveland the most important ironstone mining district in Victorian and Edwardian Britain. The Loftus Mine was worked from 1865 to 1958 and was the third largest in the Cleveland District, employing in its heyday over 500 men and boys. Open April to early November.

Dolaucothi Gold Mine
www.nationaltrust.org.uk/dolaucothi-gold-mines tel: 01558 650177
Pumsaint, Llanwrda, SA19 8US
Located between Lampeter and Llandovery in the heart of Wales, the Dolaucothi Gold Mine is a unique mining experience, giving visitors the opportunity to walk back in time underground in a mine which has been worked since the time of the Romans. Separate guided tours throughout the day explore either the Victorian workings or the Roman workings.

Geevor Tin Mine Museum
www.geevor.com tel: 01736 788662 Pendeen, Penzance, Cornwall, TR19 7EW
The huge 67-acre Geevor site is one of the largest surviving tin mining complexes in Europe. The many listed buildings on the site are much as they were left when the mine ceased production in the 1990s, and the underground tour – led by ex-miners – takes visitors from twentieth century mining back to the eighteenth century and gives a real sense of the conditions experienced by the miners. The vast workings once went over a mile out under the sea, but are now largely inaccessible due to flooding. Open daily except, surprisingly, Saturdays.

King Edward Mine Museum
www.kingedwardmine.co.uk tel: 01209 614681 Troon, Camborne Cornwall, TR14 9DP
At the award-winning King Edward Mine there are demonstrations of Edwardian machinery from when this was a working Cornish tin mine. The exhibits tells how this mine has survived almost intact for over 100 years. Visitor see how the mine complex developed and then are taken on a guided tour of the rare equipment from the early 1900s. Much of the machinery in the mill (where tin ore is processed) is amongst the last of its kind in the world. Open every day except Tuesdays and Fridays in September.

Morwellham Quay
www.morwellham-quay.co.uk tel: 01822 832766 Morwellham, Tavistock Devon PL19 8JL
An award-winning World Heritage Site, featuring a historic port and copper mine. Visitors can travel by train along the banks of the River Tamar before venturing deep underground in the George & Charlotte copper mine. Here, in their abandoned workplaces, displays illustrate the harsh working conditions of Victorian miners. Inside the mine visitors see copper ore seams and the fully working water wheel used to pump water from the lower levels. Open daily. Admission charge.

Museum of Lead Mining Wanlockhead
www.leadminingmuseum.co.uk tel: 01659 74387
The Museum of Lead Mining Wanlockhead, by Biggar, Lanarkshire ML12 6UT
Developed around an 18th century lead mine set deep in the hillside – where visitors can experience the thrill of going underground – the museum celebrates an industry which once dominated the area. There are two miners' cottages recreating how miners lived, and the second oldest subscription Library in Europe, which has recently gained Recognition status as being a collection of National Significance. Nearby is the Wanlockhead Beam Engine, and other relics of lead mining's industrial past.

North of England Lead Mining Museum
www.killhope.org.uk tel: 01388 537505
Near Cowshill, Upper Weardale, Co. Durham, DL13 1AR
Killhope is a fully restored nineteenth century lead mine, celebrating the life and work of the lead mining families of the Pennines. On site is a huge working waterwheel. Visitors can experience the miners' living conditions, work as a 'washerboy' looking for galena – lead ore. In the 'jigger house' is a collection of working machinery. Killhope also offers the opportunity to take a mine tour. Park Level Mine was reopened to the public in 1996. Open daily April to early November.

Peak District Mining Museum
www.peakmines.co.uk tel: 01629 583834 South Parade, Matlock, Derbyshire DE4 3NR
In the unexpected setting of the former Pavilion in Matlock Bath, the museum includes a recreation of a lead mine, and many artefacts and displays exploring the history of lead mining in the area. Open daily. Across the road is Temple Mine, also part of the museum, and underground tours are arranged at noon and 1400.

Sygun Copper Mine
www.syguncoppermine.co.uk tel: 01766 890595 Beddgelert Gwynedd LL55 4NE
The self-guided underground audio tour of this spectacular mine in the heart of the Snowdonia National Park takes the visitor back in time to the heart of the Victorian copper mine, through winding tunnels and into large spectacular caverns, where the seams of copper can still be seen – some of them containing gold and silver as well as other precious metals. Open daily from early March to the end of October.

Yorkshire Dales Mining Museum
www.yorkshiredalesminingmuseum.com tel:01282 841422
Old Grammar School, School Lane, Earby, Barnoldswick, Lancs BB18 6QF
The museum includes a reconstructed horse level with Dales Pony "Kexwith Bess" drawing out a rake of three wagons. Upstairs pickmen are working a lead vein and filling the ore into small cars known as durk wagons to be tipped into an orepass feeding a hopper in the horse level below. As well as the tableaux there are comprehensive displays of tools, photographs and memorabilia illustrating the mining, dressing and smelting of lead ore. Open summer Sundays.

The shell of the engine house is all that remains of the tin mine at Towanwroath, Cornwall.

INDEX

Page numbers in italics denote illustrations